In Harm s Way

by Vernon Scott

For the boys of North Road School, Milford Haven,
with whom I shared the perils and excitement
of the summer of 1940

Published by
PATERCHURCH PUBLICATIONS
6 Laws Street, Pembroke Dock
Pembrokeshire, SA72 6DL
Tel: 01646 683041

First Printed: November 2000

© Vernon Scott, 2000

Design and print by CIT Brace Harvatt,
Merlins Bridge, Haverfordwest.

ISBN: 1 870745 10 8

FOREWORD

I welcome the opportunity to write the foreword to this book as I was, some four decades later, to be in command of a similar major oil tank fire at a refinery on the north shore of Milford Haven, but a "Pembrokeshire Mile" from the site of the 1940 inferno at Llanreath.

This is an engrossing story, told in a most readable way. It details the personal experiences of local people and, through their recollections, relates their long hard struggle, in a variety of roles, to quell an inferno that threatened to engulf an entire community. It was to be the largest fire of its type experienced anywhere in Britain throughout the whole war.

Initially, the battle was unequal. Volunteer brigades equipped and trained primarily for peacetime domestic and rural fires, were at that early stage, ill prepared for such major wartime conflagrations. Those with memories of first hand experience, vividly recall that the early lack of equipment and water was more than compensated for by the Herculean efforts and raw courage of those sent to tame the monster. Never in their wildest imagination, did they ever envisage anything quite so awesome and frightening as it presented.

Sadly, the book also recounts the tragic deaths of five auxiliary firefighters from Cardiff who, with crews from throughout the Principality, had been mobilised to West Wales to assist their, by then, exhausted colleagues.

The book also contains lighter moments associated with the summer of 1940, and these are documented in the inimitable style of the author.

The story has to be read against the background of tremendous progress which has since been made in fire-fighting technology and modern day appliances, none of which were available to the firemen of 60 years ago. They had to rely on the basics – guts and cold water.

R. King
OBE., O. St.J., Q.F.S.M., F. I. Fire E.
Chief Fire Officer,
Mid and West Wales Fire Brigade.

INTRODUCTION

In June and July 1980, to mark the 40th anniversary of the raid, I wrote a series of articles about the bombing of the Admiralty oil tanks depot at Llanreath, Pembroke Dock.

These were subsequently serialised in the *Western Telegraph*, and later that year published in booklet form under the title *'Inferno 1940'*. A substantial number of local firemen who fought the blaze, together with others associated with the drama which unfolded within the depot and elsewhere, were interviewed at length and the vividness and immediacy with which they recalled their experiences was impressive. Theirs was a story of courage and tenacity unsurpassed in the modern history of Pembrokeshire.

Since then much new evidence has come to light, along with a number of stunning photographs, which prompted an old friend and fellow author, John Evans of *Paterchurch Publications*, to suggest that perhaps the time was opportune for a bigger and more elaborate work, especially as the year 2000 is the 60th anniversary of the assault against the tanks.

This book is the outcome. It differs from the modest original which dealt exclusively with the raid. On this occasion I have endeavoured to recreate what life was like for the people of Pembrokeshire that long ago summer when Britain suddenly found itself alone against what then was the world's greatest military power – Nazi Germany. *'In Harm's Way'* tells the story of some of those people, a story enriched by anecdotes both humorous and tragic. They were mostly ordinary men and woman, living through an extraordinary time.

A peculiar mood prevailed throughout the nation in 1940. It is somewhat difficult to describe now; suffice to say daily fear and tension gradually gave way to a single-minded determination that produced many acts of selfless heroism and sacrifice.

For this new account I am indebted to the staff of the County Records Office, especially Marie Lewis, for providing access to copies of the *West Wales Guardian* and *Western Telegraph* for the summer of 1940. It should be noted that after initial reference to the first named newspaper by its full title, thereafter it becomes the *Guardian*. Similarly, the *Western Telegraph* becomes the *Telegraph*.

My gratitude also goes to the following kind folk who so readily came forward with their memories of that year, and who loaned photographs: Lord Parry of Neyland; Henry and Myra Jones, Fishguard; John and Maureen Arter, St Davids; Ewan Jenkins, Solva; Keith Parsons, Marloes; Raymond Evans, Mike George, Milford Haven; Bill Richards, Ted Goddard, Haverfordwest; Fred Dyson, formerly of Creature Farm, Bosherston, now of Pembroke Dock; Dennis Alderman, Castlemartin; John James, Mellaston; Mrs Doris James, Freestone Cross, Cresselly; Mrs

Doris English, Tenby; Bryan Phillips, Mrs Joyce Baldwin, Pembroke; Mrs Betty Lomas, Mrs Jean Parkinson, Mrs Joan Davey, Mrs Pat Phillips, Mrs Mary Owens, Mrs Nancy Thomas, Ted Owens, Roy Hordley and John Worley, Pembroke Dock, and Andy Stevens, Bristol. Because of my infallible memory some names may have been inadvertently omitted, for which I apologise in advance. All of the firemen who provided information for 'Inferno' are mentioned in this book which, I trust, will serve as a tribute to their memory. Very few are left now.

I am especially grateful to Mr Ronnie King, Chief Fire Officer, Mid and West Wales Fire Brigade, for writing the foreword. Mr King has always taken a keen interest in the oil tanks fire and attends the annual memorial service.

My thanks also to John Evans, *Paterchurch Publications*, for his encouragement, support and advice, and to Tim Adams, Neil Davies, Phil Davies and the staff of CIT Brace Harvatt, Haverfordwest, for their expertise and cheerful co-operation.

Let us now then, recall the sights and sounds of 60 years ago; let us drift back through the mists of time to the most decisive summer of the 20th century – the summer of 1940.

Vernon Scott
Pembroke Dock
November 2000

By the same author:
INFERNO 1940 (1980)
AN EXPERIENCE SHARED 1939-1945 (1992; reprinted 1993)
WHEN THE POPPIES BLOOM AGAIN
    Pembrokeshire and the Great War (1998)

CHAPTER ONE

MAY – JUNE

"If we fail..."

The Battle of France is over. I expect the Battle of Britain is about to begin. The whole fury and might of the enemy must very soon be turned on us. Hitler knows he will have to break us in this island or lose the war. If we can stand up to him, all Europe may be free and the life of the world may move forward into broad sunlit uplands. But if we fail, then the whole world, including the United States, including all that we have known and cared for, will sink into the abyss of a new Dark Age, made more sinister and perhaps, more protracted, by the lights of perverted science. Let us, therefore, brace ourselves to our duties and so bear ourselves that if the British Empire and its Commonwealth last for a thousand years, men will say "This was their finest hour."

Winston Churchill, June 18th 1940.

Following Churchill's appointment on May 10th as Prime Minister in succession to the discredited Neville Chamberlain, the new leader warned he had nothing to offer except "Blood, toil, tears and sweat," a stark message best understood near the end of the month by the British Expeditionary Force as it fought a desperate rearguard action around Dunkirk.

The subsequent evacuation from the beaches there, codenamed "Operation Dynamo," was completed by June 4th, 338,000 troops having been rescued and brought home. Among local RAF veterans who eventually arrived on convalescence leave was George Tasker from the South Pembrokeshire village of Cresselly. He was nowhere near Dunkirk, being an RAF survivor of what was to be the greatest maritime disaster of the war – the sinking of the Cunard – White Star liner *Lancastria* on Monday June 17th off St Nazaire. The 16,243 ton ship had successfully evacuated 9,000 members of the BEF along with a number of French civilians, and was preparing to depart for Southampton when she was attacked by a large force of German bombers. Carnage followed; *Lancastria*, a sitting duck, sank within 30 minutes and several thousand were either killed during the vicious assault or perished through drowning.

Churchill knew full well the devastating affect this catastrophe would have on the nation's already battered morale, so a news blackout was imposed and the full horrific facts did not emerge until some time after the war. Survivors, like RAF man George Tasker, were ordered not to talk about the tragedy, and their lips remained sealed throughout the conflict.

Following the fall of France, Pembrokeshire, like every part of Britain, was awash with rumour, and news of German forces massing across the Channel for an imminent invasion led to the tightening of existing security measures and the introduction of new ones, which included a ban on the use of binoculars by civilians without official permission.

Those who continued to contravene blackout regulations were severely dealt with at hastily convened courts, and at Milford Sessions in the second week of May a keen amateur photographer, 30 year old Albert Charles Williams, Chapel Street, Hakin, was fined £3 for "making a photograph of a seaplane without permit from the Secretary of State for War". Mr Williams pleaded guilty, but pointed out that at the time he was snapping a Dutch Fokker seaplane, newly arrived at RAF Pembroke Dock, he had no idea the law was being broken. This was the first case of its kind in Pembrokeshire, and the court chairman warned that in future the maximum penalty for such an offence would be £100, or three months imprisonment.

In an editorial on May 24th a local paper, the *West Wales Guardian*, declared "Since the development of the terrible holocaust on the Western Front, innumerable rumours have gained currency in Pembroke and Pembroke Dock. There are stories of well known local people being killed in action in France; of the landing of German troops in remote creeks on the South Pembrokeshire coast; of Fifth Columnists and parachutists. Forunately most people have sense enough to realise that stories of this kind are figments of somebody's imagination." What the writer failed to concede was that such scaremongering always had to be investigated, much to the inconvenience of the military and police.

There was no shortage of volunteers in the county to join the L. D. V. (Local Defence Volunteers), almost immediately re-named the Home Guard. This organisation was formed not very long before Dunkirk, and within six weeks a staggering 1,400,000 men had enlisted nationwide. In its early days some people unkindly labled the L. D. V. the "Look, duck, and vanish brigade!" but it became a force to be reckoned with.

Not all of its recruits fitted the "Dad's Army" image.

Dai Owens of Pennar, Pembroke Dock, was just 17 and first to join the town's unit, along with his brother-in-law, Harry Gibby, and a close friend, Billy Thomas. They were also 17. In later years Dai recalled urgent knocking on the door of his home in the early hours of a June morning in 1940 and the caller, Lieutenant Percy Castle, second-in-command of the Pembroke Dock Home Guard, yelling "Grab your rifle! The Germans have come!" Dai added "I rushed around in pitch darkness to rouse Billy and Harry, and we hurried to our designated defence position in a field at Golden Hill, Pembroke. We had only been given very sketchy information, the crux of which was that Germans had been seen coming ashore on a local beach. To say we were apprehensive is an understatement; it was light by 4am and the birds were singing and chirping. I remember thinking

Called out to combat German parachutists! Dai Owens (left), and close friend Billy Thomas, who joined the Pembroke Dock Home Guard at the age of 17.

(Mrs Mary Owens)

'Why are the Jerries spoiling a lovely morning like this!' I also felt deep concern for my family, as did my companions. There was much relief all round when the order came to 'stand down' at 5am. It was sheepishly explained the whole thing had been a false alarm, which led to much grumbling and cursing on the part of the men. With hindsight though, the experience didn't do us any harm".

Three members of the Castlemartin Home Guard, Sergeant Cyril Watkins and Privates John James and Ivor Thomas, spent several nervous nights "defending" the sprawling beach at Freshwater West, just outside the entrance to Milford Haven on the southern side.

John James remembered "We were issued with former American Army 300 rifles dating back to 1914 – where they came from I don't know – and carried three rounds each and a bayonet. We were scared stiff, and could see enemy landing barges on every wave! To be honest, if Germans troops had come I do believe we'd have run like hell!"

At Milford, on a Sunday, information was received that parachutists had been sighted descending into picturesque Hilton Woods, near Black Bridge, and brothers Billy and Freddie Laugharne, next door neighbours in Pill Lane, were among a Home Guard platoon sent to investigate.

"When we got there we fanned out and conducted a thorough search, but apart from some courting couples and children picking flowers, saw no one else", said Billy. "This was just as well because at that stage we were inadequately trained, poorly equipped and wouldn't have stood a chance against enemy troops. It was a time of much tension; everybody was jittery because the Germans were expected to invade in force any day".

Ron Hicks of the Carew and District platoon, Home Guard, said that when members were eventually kitted out with uniforms, they paraded carrying pick-axe handles and broomsticks.

Boys of the Old Brigade! In 1989 the only known survivors of the Carew and District Home Guard Platoon came together for this photograph. Left to right are, back: Harry Roberts, Hugh Williams, Maurice Griffiths, Hubert Williams; middle: Tom Cole, Ashley Griffiths, George Davies, Harry Thomas; front: Ron Hicks, Evan "Ianto" Perkins, George and Billy Brace. "Corporal" Perkins, then 91, was one of the small raiding party who spirited away the commanding officer's alcohol supply in the summer of 1940! (Mrs Doris James)

"They were our only form of armament and God knows how we would have repulsed the enemy had they parachuted into our midst because invasion was all the talk then. We didn't get rifles until later and, even then, some time elapsed before ammunition arrived".

The exploits of this platoon during the summer of 1940 and indeed, for the rest of the war, were to become part of local folk-lore. Ianto Perkins, who was a corporal, recalled "In the last week of June 1940, we were advised that strangers were spying on the airfield at RAF Carew Cheriton. Strangers in civilian clothing stuck out like a sore thumb in rural areas, and we were ordered to search for such persons and, if need be, take them into police custody. At the same time we got wind of the fact that, in readiness for a social meeting with regular army officers, our commanding officer, Captain Tom Scourfield, had taken delivery of a large supply of alcohol which was stored in his garden shed. So while most of us went searching for spies, a small commando-type party made up of Will and Albert Harries, 'Tailor' Cole and myself, mounted a daring raid on the shed and got away with the captain's booze! Talk about putting military training to good use! At the following evening's parade, Tom instructed us to keep our ears to the ground because some buggers had pinched his beer and spirits! Our straight faces did us proud! There were a lot of rumours flying around then, especially about enemy agents, but I can't remember anyone being picked up for spying in our area".

Rumours affected the whole county and at Llanrhian in the north, schoolmaster Bryn Davies, who was also the village's ARP (Air Raid Precaution) warden, asked pupil Ewan Jenkins to dash a mile or so down the road with a written message for a group of local women preparing accommodation for evacuees due to arrive from London. The message warned them to be on their guard and act with the utmost caution because he (Mr Davies) had been advised by a highly reliable source that German forces were in the seaside village of Saundersfoot!

Who spread such tales? Some were irresponsible youngsters, as was evidenced by the court appearance of a 16 year old lad who, according to the *Guardian*... "Insisted that he'd seen two parachutists land near Trewent, Freshwater East, on a recent Sunday". It was stated that a considerable number of regular police and special constables were called out to make a thorough search of the area, wasting many hours in the process. The boy eventually admitted making the whole thing up. Pembroke magistrates took a dim view of this behaviour and he was fined £3 and sternly reprimanded.

Such mischief took different forms. A boy aged 15 appeared before a juvenile court at Mathry, charged with ringing one of the bells in St Davids Cathedral. It was the first charge in Pembrokeshire, under the Defence Regulations, of a bell being rung without instruction from an authorised person. The boy, a former pupil of St Davids County School, admitted the offence.

Police Sergeant Idwal Evans said members of the special constabulary, ARP personnel and Local Defence Volunteers had answered the bell, believing it to be a warning that enemy parachutists had landed. The officer added "Many people came running on to the streets at St Davids, and some women were on the verge of collapse". The boy, fined £1 with three months to pay, received a dressing down from the court chairman and was told " You are too big for pranks like this and must realise your responsibilities".

But not all the rumours stemmed from "pranks". That the Germans had agents in Pembrokeshire during the war has never been in doubt. Broadcasts by the traitor William Joyce, 'Lord Haw-Haw', contained such accurate accounts of enemy air raids on Pembroke Dock that they could only have come from sources in the area at the time. Joyce even named streets in the town destroyed by bombing.

Farm worker Charlie Howells, Nurses Cottage, Warren, saw a man taking photographs close to the army's tank-training range at Castlemartin, and tipped off the local constable who arrested the person. Some days later police officers called to thank Charlie, mentioning that when they searched the man's living accommodation in Tenby, they came across evidence which suggested he was a spy.

Some years ago an elderly German couple spent a caravan holiday at Solva, North Pembrokeshire, and became friendly with professional artist Keith Parsons, whose home is in Marloes. He was also enjoying a holiday break at Solva. During the course of their conversations, the husband revealed he was a former U-boat captain visiting Pembrokeshire to see what Pointz Castle beach, near Brawdy, looked like in daylight! Mr Parsons told the author "He confided that on a number of occasions his boat surfaced off the coastline to re-charge its batteries and send crewmen ashore for fresh water. There is a spring at Pointz Castle which the Germans used. The beach there is isolated, so it would have been an ideal spot to land after dark". Which begs the question – who advised the Germans about the spring in the first place?

A torch flash from Pointz Castle beach or the cliff top, would have signalled the go-ahead for U-boat personnel to come in by dinghy and make their way stealthily to the spring and – who knows – elsewhere? Almost certainly, enemy agents would have been ferried ashore or taken off during some of these secret sojourns. The U-boat veteran indicated to Mr Parsons that his clandestine visits were made early in the war, so it is ironic that while allegations regarding German infiltrators in the summer of 1940 proved, after investigation, to be nothing more than rumours, enemy sailors were actually landing on a deserted beach without anyone being aware!

In late June there was a number of weddings involving airmen from the RAF's flying boat station at Pembroke Dock and local girls, who included Gladys Wilcox, Edith Maud Dew and Eleanor Hannah James, Pembroke Dock, and Margaret Audrey Elmes and Grace Seabourne of Pembroke.

The *Guardian* referred to the unfortunate circumstances surrounding the wedding of another couple, stating "With wailing air raid sirens replacing the traditional joyous wedding bells, with bridesmaids, wedding cake, and even the bride's white satin gown dispensed with owing to the exigencies of war, the marriage was solemnised at Folkstone last week of Corporal William Henry Thomas, RAF, third son of Mrs and the late Mr N. Thomas, Syfnau Cottage, Rosebush, and Miss Mildred Joan Wallace, daughter of Mr and Mrs W. E. Wallace, 18 Castle Street, Pennar, Pembroke Dock.

"They had planned to marry in Pembroke Dock in the near future; every arrangement had been made and a colossal wedding cake, decorated with miniature aeroplanes and RAF-blue icing, had arrived. The bride had ordered her white satin gown, and chosen two of her friends as bridesmaids. But when all was ready the grimness of war made its presence felt, the bridegroom being suddenly posted from RAF Pembroke Dock. Possessed of the true British spirit however, the couple were not easily dismayed and a few days later were reunited at Folkstone, marrying there without delay.

"Her gown left behind in Pembroke Dock, the bride wore a grey ensemble with hat and shoes to tone, and a spray of carnations. The bridesmaids, Miss Betty Scourfield and Miss Lorna McGregor, were unable to be present owing to the emergency arrangements. Shortly after the ceremony air raid sirens sounded and the newly weds, along with hundreds of others, had to rush for shelter. Nor was a peaceful honeymoon to be theirs, for during the short leave the 'groom obtained, there were several air raids".

A Tenby columnist in the local *Guardian*, known as *"The Gossip"*, described the scrapping of an air raid shelter on the town's South Parade as "inevitable".

He contended "A more unsuitable place than this centuries-old archway could not have been selected for such a purpose. From the time when the first sheet of corrugated metal was fixed, it was ridiculed and condemned. It is significant that troops in the town mistook the shelter for a toilet and used it accordingly. It was only last year that a portion of this arch collapsed and had to be repaired by the corporation, yet it was considered suitable as a protection from enemy bombing ! It is really a pity the council ever sanctioned its selection as a public shelter. Now the menace of air raids is developing into stark reality, complacency in official quarters is giving place to grave apprehension. This was reflected in the local council chamber last week when at last members came to grips with the subject". (At this meeting it was decided that in addition to approaching Pembrokeshire's MP, Major Gwilym Lloyd George, the council should immediately get in touch with the Ministry for Home Security with regard to the provision of Anderson outdoor shelters).

"The Gossip" also had this to say about the increasing number of evacuees arriving daily in the county... "It is rather surprising to find a correspondent in the press advocating the evacuation of the children of

Pembrokeshire to safe homes in Devonshire before they are exposed to terrible risk and danger from air raids. Remembering that during the last fortnight hundreds of children have been brought here from the south and east coasts of England, the government must have considered they would be safe in Pembrokeshire. It certainly must strike one as extraordinary, therefore, that a proposal to move them again should have been made almost before they had time to settle down..."

Not only kiddies were being shuttled about from the threat of aerial bombardment, it being announced that a quarter of a million sheep had been evacuated from the Sussex coast. They belonged to a famous strain which had long been bred on Romney Marsh.

Reading the local press, men and women home on leave from the forces must have been startled at the way war news was often overshadowed by what, to them, seemed trivial matters. A fair amount of space was given to the discovery a short distance from St Ishmaels vicarage, near Milford Haven, of a six foot long stone coffin. It was unearthed by workmen digging a trench and found to contain the skeleton of a man, with the bottom set of teeth in an excellent state of preservation! The remains, believed to be many centuries old, were passed into the custody of the vicar, the Rev Gordon Williams.

At Milford Sessions Peglers Stores Ltd, Charles Street, were summoned by the Food Executive Officer (Mr Horace L. Howarth, who was also the town clerk), for selling 6 lb of sugar to Mrs Ruby Scurlock, Biggins Hill House, Waterston, this being in excess of the rationed quantity.

The court heard the case arose following a complaint lodged by a person whose name was not disclosed. Prosecuting solicitor, Mr F. E. Greathead, Pembroke, reminded magistrates that the sugar ration was 12 ounces per person and in this instance 6 lb was supplied to a household of only four persons – twice the proper quantity. It was submitted that this supply was held out as a bait by Peglers Ltd to induce the customer concerned to purchase further goods.

After a lengthy hearing the case was dismissed on the grounds the prosecution had not made a satisfactory case. Mr J. E. P. Morris, for Peglers, asserted "We are not under the Gestapo at Milford, thank God! We have not been told who the informant was. The whole thing savours of persecution rather than prosecution".

Workmen "leaning on their brushes instead of doing a decent day's work" were condemned at a meeting of Pembroke Borough Council. Members reacted angrily when the surveyor, Mr P. Morgan, suggested another man be taken on. Councillor George complained the workmen were not carrying out their duties as they should, and Alderman Hay said they took no interest in their work and were only putting in time.

The chairman, Alderman W. J. Gwilliam, observed "With these men it seems a case of 'Come day, go day, God send Sunday!' If they won't get on with their work then we must get someone else who will". The surveyor said he would investigate the complaints.

At the same meeting Councillor Galloway, chairman of the sanitary committee, warned that Pembroke's rat population was fast increasing and immediate steps should be taken to stop the plague.

This prompted Alderman Gwilliam to retort "We cannot wage war on Pembroke's rats for one week and declare an armistice for the remaining 51! If we are to rid ourselves of rats we must keep at it". Councillor Galloway said places where food scraps were left were the most infected, and it was agreed steps be taken to clear such areas of stale food and that baits be laid.

The many devotees of the *Guardian's* naturalist, H. R. Chubb, were intrigued to read in June that he had adapted his monthly column to suit the war.

Under the heading "A Light That Still Shines In The Blackout," Chubb, a railwayman at Goodwick, pointed out that the black-out regulations were entirely ignored by the glow-worm..." whose light shines brightly in the darkness of these wartime nights. Sometimes the glow-worm's light, gleaming steadily in the night, draws the fire of a sentry, but continues to shine defiantly to the complete mystification of its attacker ".

What did the boys and girls home on leave make of that?

An aerial view of Pembroke Dock in the late 1930s. The Llanreath oil tanks depot is in the top right corner of the picture. The very large area of land stretching

away from the tanks is the Barracks Hill. Scores of women and children were blackberrying there at the time of the August 19th air raid.

CHAPTER TWO
JULY – AUGUST
"The utmost dissatisfaction exists..."

The first actual raid occurred this morning. The children remained in school and took cover beneath the desks. Community singing kept them happy and there was no panic. Both staff and children behaved splendidly. Teachers have resolved to work extra time to make windows more protective by covering them with net.
Entry in the log book of Albion Square Girls and Infant School,
Pembroke Dock, July 10th.

On May 4th Adolf Hitler issued the following directive: "Apart from operations in France, the Luftwaffe is authorised to attack the British homeland in the fullest manner as soon as sufficient forces are available".

Following the French capitulation, Germany swiftly established airfields in that country and utilised existing ones, so that in a matter of days no part of the British Isles was beyond the reach of the Luftwaffe. Locally, shipping off the West Wales coast was harassed with increasing frequency, and on the morning of July 10th the inevitable happened, a Pembrokeshire town – Pembroke Dock – was bombed.

The local press, printing heavily censored details, said the incident involved a single aircraft which circled a West Wales town for almost half an hour, dropping three or four bombs. It was claimed that only slight damage was done and there were no casualties. The report added "An air raid warning was sounded but only a few people in the town heard it. A little later there came another explosion followed by the rattle of machine-gun fire. Many people saw two bombs drop from an aircraft flying at a great height, and it is thought they fell into the sea. The first bomb fell at 10. 12am and the 'All Clear' sounded at 10.50am". The raid was carried out by two Ju 88s (Junkers 88s), and a total of 12 heavy explosives were dropped. Two fell within the Admiralty oil tanks complex at Llanreath but, as luck would have it, failed to explode. One which came to rest on top of a tank was made safe, and the other caused a leak in a tank containing 164,800 gallons of oil. Of the remaining bombs, one fell in the harbour between Pembroke Dock and Neyland, and the rest on open ground around Llanreath. It transpired that the machine-gun heard was used by soldiers to fire at the aircraft.

This raid dramatically demonstrated that Pembrokeshire was now very much in harm's way, especially Pembroke Dock with its various military targets. Arthur Morris, the town's experienced and highly thought of fire chief, warned his men that with no anti-aircraft defence in the area, and none anticipated in the foreseeable future, Pembroke Dock could expect attacks on a more determined scale. He added gravely "If they go for the oil tanks again – as they surely will – all I can say is God help us!"

H.R. "Taff" Morgan (who later settled in the town) was serving with the RAF at Pembroke Dock when the first aerial assault took place. He recalled "As ground crews we had settled into a routine, servicing and repairing the flying boats, seeing them off on patrol and looking forward to their safe return. Ground tradesmen were detailed to meet each flying boat as it landed and carry out whatever essential servicing was required.

"This duty commenced at about 6pm and continued for the better part of the night. I had been on such a shift on the beautiful moonlit night of July 9th – 10th, finishing work and coming ashore in the pinnace at dawn. Our crew was billeted on the ground floor of one of the barrack blocks and

Part of a "spy-in-the-sky" photograph of Pembroke Dock taken from a German reconnaissance aircraft in late May 1940. This picture was subsequently issued to Luftwaffe aircrews in target-map form and copies were carried by the Ju 88 pilots who bombed the Llanreath tanks. The tanks, labeled B in the left foreground, were only a small part of the military set-up at Pembroke Dock. Other installations included the Royal Navy base and RAF flying-boat anchorage and hangarage (marked C and D); radio stations (F 1 and F 2), and army barracks (E and G). There was also another Admiralty oil tanks depot at Llanion, top right. Despite the importance of Pembroke Dock as a joint service base, the town was completely undefended in the summer of 1940. (Author's Collection)

we awoke around 9.45am. One of the boys brought in a couple of pots of tea, and we were sitting on our beds drinking and having a natter, when there came the drone of aircraft engines, the sound of which was totally unfamiliar to us.

"Suddenly there was an almighty bang, followed by a number of thuds, and the night shift, as one and in a variety of attire, dived out of the open windows and shot off to the nearest air raid shelter! We found out later that some of the bombs had straddled the Barracks Hill, right behind the flying boat base. When we eventually emerged from the shelter, someone said 'Well chaps, that's it! The war has come to P.D!' "

RAF personnel were lucky to have fortified shelters available when the enemy was overhead, because the civilian population had no such facility. At a packed public meeting in Pembroke Dock on the evening of July 12th, the Rev J.T. Morgan, Curate of St Patrick's Church, Pennar, and a man well known for his forthright approach to matters, angrily complained there was a deplorable lack of air raid shelters in the town; he considered the fault for this rested at the door of the local council. Who else could they look to besides their duly elected representatives on Pembroke Borough Council? No one !

In his opinion explanations given by councillors were very lame, and he felt strong representation should be made to the local authority expressing surprise and deep concern at the lack of shelter provision. Personally, he did not think the people of Pembroke Dock would panic in an air raid; they would be frightened of course, but there would be no panic.

Councillor J. R. Williams assured all present that the council was giving ARP matters the greatest consideration, and Councillor W. J. Phillips pointed out that it had now been decided to erect shelters in various parts of Pembroke Dock and neighbouring Pembroke for the benefit of those caught on the streets when a raid was in progress. A well known local personality, Mr Ted Sherlock, said he spoke as one who had experienced air raids in the 1914-18 War, and could assure Pembroke Dock residents that aerial bombardment was not so dreadful as it was made out to be. The chances of being hit were one in a million. Twelve months on, those words would come back to haunt this gentlemen.

Councillor John Rhys Williams, one of the more eloquent and outspoken members of Pembroke Borough Council, was known to all by his initials – 'J.R.' Short, sturdily built and always brimming with confidence, he arrived in Pembroke Dock from his native Cwmavon a year or two before the war to become secretary of the town's Rechabite Society. He soon won a place on the council and quickly became a household name, being widely regarded as a champion of the underdog. He also had a keen eye for headlines, and was on close and harmonious terms with the local press, who valued him as a good and reliable news contact.

Following further hit and run raids on Pembroke Dock in July,

*Councillor John Rhys Williams
– the irrepressible 'J.R'! He
warned that Pembroke Dock
was in harm's way.
(Western Telegraph).*

including the first night attack, 'J. R.', without mentioning the town by name, had this to say in a letter to the *Guardian*:

"Air raid precautions in so far as providing warning of an impending air raid is concerned, have had their first real tests recently, and it is regrettable to have to state that in one town the utmost dissatisfaction exists at what was left undone. Up to the time of writing, on no occasion has the public air raid siren given warning, the first indication of danger being the sound of exploding bombs. It is true that immediately after the explosions a siren was sounded, but this was not the public siren and being less powerful, was not heard by a large number of people. (The other siren referred to was at the RAF flying boat station).

"To say the least, the knowledge bombs may drop on the town without any warning whatever, has caused a great deal of uneasiness. If it is true that local officials have to wait for authority from elsewhere before sounding the warning, then it is time there was a drastic revision of arrangements. Surely every town should be allowed to act on its own initiative? Is it not better to have half a dozen false alarms in a day, than an unexpected air raid in which a score of people may be killed because of lack of warning?"

There was not a person in Pembroke Dock who did not agree with those sentiments, as was evidenced by letters of support in the next issue of the *Guardian*. It was revealed in that edition that Chief Stoker William John Henry Phillips, son of Mr and Mrs Griff Phillips, Newport Road, Fishguard, had been awarded the OBE (Military Division) for courage and devotion to duty when fire broke out in the boiler-room of the sloop *HMS Bideford*. This was the only good news on a front page dominated by an ever increasing list of Pembrokeshire boys who had been killed in France, or were missing in action.

Perhaps these sad tidings were partly responsible for desertion on the part of a small number of soldiers from locally based units, about which the *Guardian* also reported. In one such case Daniel David Drinkwater, Royal Army Medical Corps, appeared in custody at a Pembroke Dock court charged with being a deserter. Police Sergeant Bodman gave evidence of finding Drinkwater in a house in Imble Street, Pembroke Dock, and after being questioned he admitted being absent without leave. But the errant soldier asserted "It was my honest intention to return to barracks; I heard someone singing 'There'll Always be an England' and that made me pull myself together, and determine to rejoin my unit". The defendant was remanded to await a military escort.

In the issue of Friday July 19th the *Guardian's* H. R. Chubb was at it again, the contents of his nature notes reading: "One of the diabolical products of the present war is the 'screaming bomb', of which a number of us already have some experience. When the missile is released by an enemy 'plane, it falls quickly to earth and its velocity produces a high pitched whistle or scream which rises to a crescendo as the bomb nears the ground.

"The device by which the scream is manufactured is probably a simple one, but its principles could no doubt be found to be somewhat similar to the rush of air through the wing feathers of a stooping falcon. The peregrine often dives from a great height at a speed of something like 150 miles an hour, and at close quarters the noise of its terrific rush to earth sounds like a miniature screaming bomb".

⸻ •⊹⦂•❖⦂❖⦂❖•⦂⊹• ⸻

Concerts organised for members of the armed forces and civilians throughout Pembrokeshire drew capacity audiences, and played an important part in maintaining and boosting morale. During the summer of 1940 some of the·most popular songs requested of artistes were *A Nightingale Sang in Berkeley Square*; *When You Wish Upon a Star*; *It's a Lovely Day Tomorrow*; *Arm and Arm Together (Just Like We Used To Be)*; *Let the People Sing*; *Our Love Affair*; *Deep Purple*; *Faithful for Ever*; *There Goes That Song Again*, and *Somewhere Over the Rainbow*.

The public also continued to enjoy songs associated with the first three months of the war, such as the one mentioned by the army deserter –

There'll Always be an England (Where There's a Country Lane). Others included *My Prayer (Is to linger with You)*; *Moonlight Serenade*, *Little Brown Jug*; *In the Mood*; *We'll Meet Again*, and *Run, Rabbit, Run.* The last named was especially popular with children!

At the cinema *Gone With the Wind* and *The Wizard of Oz* were outstanding attractions, and on the wireless *Garrison Theatre* starring Jack "Mind my bike" Warner as an army private forever flirting with snooty cinema usherette Joan Winters (Progrems, choclits, cigarettes and mep of the cemp), became enormously popular.

In less than a fortnight during July, two tons of aluminum were collected in the county town of Haverfordwest and district, sufficient to build two Spitfires for the RAF. The collection was undertaken by energetic members of the local Women's Voluntary Service (WVS) who, as soon as an appeal was made by Lord Beaverbrook, Minister of Aircraft Production, set to work with such vigor that articles of all description poured into a depot in Hill Street, Haverfordwest.

WVS centre organiser, Mrs A. V. A. Lloyd, said it was hoped to have one of the Spitfires christened "Honey Harfat" adding "and doubtless we shall be able to find a suitable name for the second!"

The glorious sunny weather of July continued into August and in Haverfordwest on the first day of the month, scores of people were said to have found peaceful seclusion along the Scotchwells Walk, the *Guardian* eulogising "In groups they sat by the refreshing waters, or in the shade of trees, evidently finding the delightful spot a refuge from the tumolt of the outer world".

On the same afternoon L. G. James, Haverfordwest Grammar School's opening batsman, scored his first century, and the team's first of the season. Batting against a team of clergymen selected by a Mr Weller, he hit a stylish 104 not out. The clergy batted first and put on 98, top scorers being the Rev Barnard Jones (22 not out), and the Rev W. Roberts (25). The school passed this total for only two wickets and afterwards piled on the runs, S. Lucas knocking up a bright 55.

The fine conditions also favoured the Luftwaffe and that evening at dusk, with scores of civilians and service personnel strolling about, a German bomb-aimer selected Llanion Barracks, Pembroke Dock, as his target. Ten bombs fell in the barracks area as an He 111 (Heinkel 111) roared across the darkening sky, and although surprisingly little damage was caused, a 20 year old soldier, Private Ronald Johnson from Manchester, was struck by shrapnel and killed. He was Pembroke Dock's first fatality of the war due to enemy action.

There were further bitter complaints that the town siren was not activated until after the bombs were dropped, and at a meeting of the borough council 24 hours later, Councillor J. R. Williams was again up in arms. He also submitted a petition signed by 58 residents of Llanreath, which called for the urgent installation of their own air raid warning siren, it being claimed there were occasions when the town siren could not be heard, and that in some parts of the village had not been heard at all.

Councillor Williams emphasised that Llanreath's very location (right next to the oil tanks site, althought reporters present were banned from writing that) made it absolutely vital residents had their own siren.

It was decided to forward the petition to the County ARP Authority, stating that the council fully supported it.

A row subsequently erupted when Councillor J. Hay referred to the proposed public air-raid shelters and asked when they were to be built? Townspeople, he said, were anxious to know. The Mayor, Councillor J. Gwyther, said powers in this matter had now been delegated to local authorities, but Councillor W. W. George pointed out this only applied to house shelters.

Councillor J. R. Williams said he had been given to understand that in Haverfordwest the public shelter programme was almost complete; he was inclined to believe Haverfordwest people received preferential treatment.

This upset Alderman F. W. Tucker, a member of the county council, who retorted angrily "I object to that remark. It is absolutely wrong".

Councillor Williams – You can object as much as you like! I am definitely of the opinion Pembroke Dock does not receive the attention it should. Unless we have the protection due to us, I shall organise a public petition in every street in Pembroke Dock and Pembroke and, if necessary, forward it to His Majesty the King, protesting against what is happening. The county authority has not been alive to our needs and indeed, it seems to me the landed gentry have to be provided for before anyone else.

Alderman Tucker – That is absolute piffle! The county council is as plebian as anyone else! I will not sit here and listen to such rot.

He then stormed out of the meeting.

Councillor J. S. James appealed to members to deal with the matter in a cool and dispassionate way, and Alderman Hay observed "When they do come to build public shelters in Pembroke Dock there'll be no bricks left – some of us are aiming them at each other all the time now!"

What could not be reported that night was Councillor J. R. Williams' correct assertion that while Pembroke Dock was very much in the line of fire, Haverfordwest which had no significant military targets, was not. The dockyard town desperately required public shelters, and he considered it grossly unfair that a substantial number had already been erected in Haverfordwest.

After the botched attempt on July 10th, Luftwaffe chiefs decided that urgent prioriity be given to a second attack against the Llanreath oil tanks. This time three

Ju 88s belonging to Kampfgruppe (Bomber Wing) 51, based at Paris – Orly, and part of the elite "Edelweiss" Kampfgeschwader (Bomber Group), would undertake the operation. The crews, hand-picked for their skill and experience, were put on standby and advised that while Pembroke Dock was without anti-aircraft gun defence, the possibility of interception by Spitfires of 92 Squadron based at RAF Pembrey, Carmarthenshire, an airfield which now formed part of the RAF's new No 10 Fighter Group, could not be ruled out. All involved with planning the operation agreed that a sudden raid pressed home with daring, determination and precision, would start a very nasty fire indeed.

Concern was expressed in Tenby over the affect enemy air activity was having on the resort's "season". In a letter to the *Guardian*, a correspondent said that on Sunday August 11th – a beautiful day – he had carefully counted the number of people on the North Beach and found it to be 384.

"The crowd", he wrote, "was composed of just over 100 soldiers, airmen and Belgium refugees, 40 children, nearly 100 local residents, and the remainder visitors. At least I assumed they were visitors, because they were certainly not Tenby people. Such figures are significant in showing how the bottom has been so completely knocked out of our 'season' ".

That couldn't have gone down well in Pembroke Dock.

(This was a case of history repeating itself. In September 1914, one month after the outbreak of the Great War, the same complaint was lodged in Tenby – that the war was spoiling the resort's "season".)

An aerial shot of Tenby taken from a Sunderland flying-boat – part of the aircraft's float can be seen on the left. It was claimed in the summer of 1940 that the war was… "spoiling Tenby's season".　　　　　　　(*John Evans Collection*)

CHAPTER THREE

AUGUST 1ST – 19TH
Countdown!

Retained firemen wanted. Must be between 25 and 35 and physically fit. Payment for attending fires: 1st hour 4/6 (four shillings and sixpence); 2nd hour 3/6; and all succeeding hours 2/6. Drills on alternate Wednesdays, for which payment of 2/6 is made. Annual retaining fee of £3 also made. Uniform free.
Milford Haven Fire Brigade advertisement in local press, August 9th.

August was an exceptionally warm month and at their monthly meeting on the evening of Tuesday the 6th, members of Pembroke Borough Fire Brigade Committee received the chairman's permission to remove their jackets before dealing with the agenda. The first item was to consider, in his absence, an application from Mr Arthur Morris for an increase in salary.

In a letter he reminded the committee that he had completed 12 months as chief officer of the Pembroke Dock Brigade at a weekly wage of three pounds, ten shillings. Since taking up the work his duties had greatly increased, and he was presently putting in 70 hours per week, not including the time when he attended fires and received no renumeration. Mr Morris also pointed out the Chief Officer at Milford, Matt Acornley, received five pounds, fifteen shillings per week inclusive, and that men of the AFS (Auxiliary Fire Service) on a full time basis, were paid three pounds, five shillings weekly, which was only five shillings less than he was earning.

Alderman Hay said it needed to be recognised that Chief Morris' workload had greatly increased, and that his duties were different from those in other Pembrokeshire towns because Pembroke as well as Pembroke Dock had to be covered. He moved that Mr Morris be paid £4 per week, and Councillor G. Jenkins seconded.

Councillor W. C. Galloway described the difficulties of running the local fire brigade at the present time, and declared "I think Mr Morris' job is very unenviable; he must be driven nearly mad with all the trouble he comes up against".

The Fire Chief was praised for his work by Councillor J. R. Williams; he was appointed before the war, and the drastic change in circumstances since then had made a great difference to the post. Mr Morris had many difficulties to contend with and moreover, not a night now passed when he wasn't called from his bed.

It was agreed to grant a wage increase of ten shillings.

A week later Chief Morris attended Pembroke Borough Council's monthly meeting to report that five Pembroke Dock AFS members had failed to respond to an alert the previous night when enemy 'planes had been in the vicinity. Four of the defaulters, Messrs John, Sillence, Rogers and Lloyd, were present and the first named told the council that he lived in the Waterloo area of the town, and was on his way to report when the "All Clear" signal was given.

"This is the first time I have failed to report. My wife was not willing for me to go and that delayed me, otherwise I would have been there", he explained.

Mr Sillence said he was en-route to the fire station when the All Clear went, adding "I put some lights out before leaving the house, and that made me a little late, but I was on my way".

Mr Rogers explained that he lived some distance away from the fire station – at Bangeston – and always took time to report. On this occasion the "All Clear" sounded before he could do so.

Mr Lloyd offered no excuse, explaining "I have a wife and three small children and had to see they were all right". He said it was also his opinion that there was insufficient protection for local firemen, and because of this he was not willing to turn out when an air raid was in progress.

The Town Clerk read a letter from the fifth man, Mr A. Skone, in which he tendered his resignation. He wrote "My wife collapsed when the siren warned of an air raid, and as this may happen again, I think it better to resign".

This was accepted, and it was agreed that Mr Lloyd be asked to tender his resignation. The explanations of the three other men were accepted.

(It should be borne in mind that few, if any, firemen owned a car in 1940 and responses were mostly made on foot. Pembroke Dock fire station was then in the Old Market House on the eastern side of the town, and within a stone's throw of the RAF flying station in the dockyard. Firemen who lived at the western end of Pembroke Dock, therefore, were faced with a lengthy sprint when the siren sounded. Bangeston, where Mr Rogers lived, is all of two miles from the Market House and Waterloo, the home of Mr John, also a fair distance away. The problem of fire brigade members leaving their wives and, in many cases small children, on their own when answering air-raid calls, was to lead to further resignations. This was why the Pembroke Dock brigade, and others in Pembrokeshire as well, began recruiting an increasing number of single men, and those with grown up families).

Midway through the month the Squire of Lamphey, Mr Ronald C. Mathias, and Mrs Shelah Mathias, Lamphey Court, near Pembroke, received confirmation from the Air Ministry that their younger son, Pilot

Officer Anthony (Tony) Ronald Mathias, had been killed in aerial action. He was posted missing on July 11th, after the Avro Anson he was piloting was shot down off the coast of Holland. He was serving with 500 Squadron at the time of his death.

Tony Mathias was 20, had been in the RAF for two years, and was engaged to Miss Thalia Henwood, Natal, South Africa, a radiologist in a London hospital. They were to have been married at Lamphey Parish Church on August 3rd. In addition to his parents he left a brother, Flight Lieutenant (later Wing Commander) Lewis Mathias, who was also an RAF pilot. He survived the war and eventually succeeded his father as Squire of Lamphey.

That same week the funeral took place of Sergeant Observer David Malpass, a 26 year old American from Scranton, Pennsylvania, who joined the RAF in the 1930s. Two days before the outbreak of war he married Miss Connie Thomas, daughter of Mr and Mrs Ben Thomas, Westgate Hill, Pembroke. After the ceremony the couple spent only a matter of hours together as the very next day the bridegroom left for France with a Blenheim squadron which formed part of the British Advanced Air Striking Force.

The irony of this sad tale is that the American survived nine months in France, during which time the ill-equipped Blenheim and Fairey Battle squadrons were practically decimated by superior enemy fighters. He returned to England and, following leave, rejoined his squadron at RAF Mildenhall, Suffolk. Connie never saw him alive again.

A few weeks later he and another observer, Sergeant Routledge, were in a Blenheim piloted by a Flying Officer Newton, who had been detailed to carry out general flying practice. Newton took off from Mildenhall aerodrome at 10.55am and at 11.30am was seen by civilian witnesses flying

KILLED IN ACTION
LAMPHEY SQUIRE'S SON

Mr. and Mrs. C. Ronald Mathias, of Lamphey Court, Pembroke, have received official information from the Air Ministry and through the Red Cross Society that their younger son, Pilot Officer Anthony (T o n y) Ronald Mathias, of the R.A.F., has been killed in action. He was posted as missing on 11th July, and the official news of his death was received last week. Pilot Officer Mathias was 20½ years of age and had been in the R.A.F. some two years. He was born at Lamphey Court and was well-known in the surrounding districts.

How the local press reported news that Pilot Officer Tony Mathias, younger son of the Squire of Lamphey, was killed in action. (John Evans Collection)

The headstone in Hundleton cemetery marking the resting place of Flight Lieutenant Cecil Halford Bull.   (John Evans)

very low over a farm which, it was later disclosed, belonged to his uncle. Before their horrified eyes, the Blenheim suddenly crashed and exploded after the starboard wing tip struck the top of a 40 foot ash tree. All the occupants were killed instantly.

Sergeant Malpass' death was a double tragedy for the Thomas family of Pembroke, because Connie's school teacher sister, Doris, was also a war widow. Her RAF husband, Corporal Ronald Wesley Ewens, was killed when Sunderland L2165 of 210 Squadron, of which he was a crew member, crashed near the entrance to Milford Haven early on September 18th 1939. It was RAF Pembroke Dock's first flying boat loss of the war, and all on board perished. Corporal Ewens and his wife met when he was posted to Pembroke Dock.

The circumstances relating to David and Connie coming together are not known; it has been suggested that he spent some time with Coastal Command at Pembroke Dock before being transferred to a land-based squadron. The American was buried in Llanion cemetery, Pembroke Dock... "so that he could be close to his wife".

Tragedy of a different kind occurred on August 8th. An RAF officer home on leave, Flight Lieutenant Cecil Halford Bull, died while shooting rabbits at Crickmarren, near Pembroke. He accidentally dropped his gun, which went off shooting him in the abdomen. He died in the arms of his distraught wife, who was with him at the time. She was the daughter of Mr and Mrs A. John, School House, Hundleton, just outside Pembroke. She and the young RAF officer, a pilot with 25 Squadron flying Blenheims, had only been married eight months.

Ambulance driver Betty Davies (later Mrs Lomas) who was taking a few hours off in Tenby when the tanks were bombed.

(Mrs Betty Lomas)

There was nothing to indicate early on Monday, August 19th, that in a matter of hours Pembroke Dock would be in the grip of fear and panic. The day, like most others throughout that golden summer, was sunny and clear and out on the placid waters of the haven twin-engined Lerwicks of 209 squadron tugged gently at their buoys in the heat haze. These graceful aircraft had arrived on July 14th from Oban, Scotland, after being temporarily relieved there by Sunderlands of 210 Squadron, Pembroke Dock.

Flying boats were a familiar sight to 32 year old engine-fitter Sid John of Llanreath, and his mates Bill James, Leslie Bevan, Will Thomas, Jack Phillips and Sid Thomas, as they crossed to Pembroke Dock on the ferry boat *Lady Magdalen* after completing another night-shift at the Royal Navy's Armament Depot, Milford Haven. There were a lot of passengers on the ferry, all earnestly discussing in small groups wireless and newspaper reports about the heroic defence being waged by RAF Fighter Command against the might of the Luftwaffe along the South Coast.

Sid John remembered someone exclaiming "Well I'll tell you one thing – Jerry will still meet bugger-all resistance if he comes back here! "People laughed, but they would have good reason to remember that remark long before the day was through.

In the kitchen of their home near the top of Beach Road, Llanreath, a weary Sid John sat down to breakfast with his wife Addie. He was concerned for her safety and that of their baby daughter Brenda, because in the first air raid of the war on Pembroke Dock the previous month, a cluster of bombs had dropped close to Llanreath, slightly damaging some properties. Everyone agreed it was a miracle there were no casualties; everyone agreed too, that the Germans were out to get the tanks, and they would surely be back.

After listening to the 9am news and hearing that every available RAF fighter had now been committed against the Luftwaffe in what Churchill was calling the Battle of Britain, Sid went to bed reminding his wife to call him at 4pm. He had always been on the punctual side and didn't want to miss the early evening ferry which linked up with the bus conveying night – shift workers to the Milford Armament Depot. As he drew the curtains he didn't give the huge Admiralty oil tanks, just 600 yards away and immediately opposite his home, a second glance.

A few doors down Mrs Annie Munro, whose husband Albert was in the army, was busy collecting clothes for the tub. It was Monday – washday. And up around the corner in Orielton Terrace, 18 year old May Tobin decided that as it was such a pleasant morning she would slip down to town to do some shopping for her mum.

By 10am the sun was so hot that Betty Davies, just turned 20, and her friend Grace Griffiths, who both lived in Military Road, not far from Llanreath, decided to catch a bus to Tenby. Betty was an ambulance driver, but felt that on such a lovely day even the Germans wouldn't be beastly enough to deny her a few hours on the beach. By the time the girls left Pembroke Dock May Tobin, daughter of a regimental sergeant major, was already ticking off her shopping list. As she strolled past the parish church of St John, she glanced at the clock tower.

It was ten past eleven.

The young woman had not the slightest inkling that by the corresponding time that night she would be staying in the vicarage, at the rear of the church, in a state of deep shock.

In a field at the top of Pennar, brothers Fred and Ron Phillips were thrashing corn, using a team of four horses. It was warm work and both men and horses were irritated by flies. Fred, his wife Eva and their children, Bryan, Joyce and David, lived in nearby Military Road but that week were staying at the holiday resort of Freshwater East, about four miles away. He left them at 7.45 that morning, and was given a lift into work by Pembroke Dock bookmaker and former professional boxer, Bill Johnson, whose own family was also holidaying at Freshwater. As he mopped his brow in the mid-day heat, Fred Phillips had no way of knowing that in a little over three hours he would become

Pembrokeshire's first civilian war casualty.

At the town's fire brigade headquarters Chief Morris was thinking about the July attack against the Llanreath oil tanks. The previous day, in conversation with a member of the army team responsible for the removal and examination of the two bombs which failed to detonate, he was told "Pembroke Dock was incredibly lucky. If the bombs had been bigger and they had exploded, you would have had one hell of a fire on your hands".

The Chief walked home for lunch wondering how much longer Pembroke Dock's luck would hold without anti -aircraft defence? It was 1pm.

Just over two hours later people at Freshwater East heard the deep, uneven throb of aircraft engines. Shielding their eyes from the glare of the afternoon sun, they could just pick out three 'planes coming in from the sea.

Some of the watchers had an uneasy feeling they were hostile.

————— • ⸱⸱=⸱ː◦⟨○◦◦ı=⸱ · • —————

One thousand feet above the wave-flecked South Pembrokeshire coastline, the pilot of the lead Ju 88 studied the target map on his lap and then alerted the crew as Pembroke Dock began to slip into vision. There wasn't a cloud over the target. Not a Spitfire nor Hurricane was in sight. The sky was theirs.

As the German airmen commenced their bomb run, they must have thought what a beautiful afternoon it was for blowing up British oil tanks.

CHAPTER FOUR

AUGUST 19TH PM
The Big Heat

What must the German airmen have thought when a tiny seaplane with a 'pusher' engine, and looking like a relic from the First World War, suddenly appeared right in front of them?...

The dramatic sequence of events that sun-drenched afternoon would remain ingrained in the memory of hundreds of people out and about in the waterfront towns of Pembroke Dock, Neyland and Milford, and of the crews manning various ships in the haven.

Among the first to spot the enemy aircraft were Skipper Albert Liffen and the men of the Milford steam trawler *Setsu*. She had been commandeered for boom defence duty at the entrance to Milford harbour, and was working on the boom which extended from Watwick Point, on the northern shore, to Angle Bay opposite.

Skipper Liffen remembered "The planes were quite high and the bright sun made it difficult to identify them properly. We were very busy at the time anyway, and didn't pay too much attention. Not very long afterwards we heard distant explosions, and saw smoke rising high into the sky in the direction of Pembroke Dock. It was obvious something serious had happened".

Unlike most trawlermen *Setsu's* skipper did not swear, and banned crew members from doing so in his presence. But he turned a deaf ear to the bad language directed against the German airmen when their aircraft re-appeared some 30 minutes later heading for the Bristol Channel.

The dive bombers had struck suddenly and with deadly effect, scoring direct hits on a tank which exploded into flame. Their pilots, confidence boosted by the lack of anti-aircraft fire and the non-appearance of RAF fighters, had flown almost leisurely up the haven to where the Texaco oil refinery now stands, and then veered south out over the open sea before turning to commence the bomb run. This took them over Freshwater East, the village of Hundleton, Pembroke River, and the Pennar and Bufferland districts of Pembroke Dock adjacent to which, on the western side, were the oil tanks.

The grief-stricken widow, other family members and RAF colleagues attending the funeral at Hundleton of Flight Lieutenant Cecil Halford Bull, accidentally killed eleven days earlier when hunting rabbits, looked up with shocked disbelief as the Ju 88s thundered low over the cemetery in turn, their nationality markings clear to the eye.

As the 'planes closed on their target, schoolboys John Arter, Mark

"In our innocence we waved back..." Mrs Jean Parkinson (left) and Mrs Joan Davey as they looked in 1940. (Mrs Jean Parkinson/Mrs Joan Davey)

Briggs, Vincent Simes, Tony Shapcott, David Furlong, Charlie Russell and Freddie Bunt, among others, were preparing to go swimming off the beach at Lower Pennar. John Arter recalled "We were close friends who always moved around in a gang, and had assembled outside my house in Ferry Road. Suddenly these planes came in fast and low, their engines drowning our conversation, and we could see the black crosses edged with white on the sides of the fuselage, and the Swastikas on the tail fins. To say we were startled is putting it mildly, because there had been no warning whatever. I clearly remember one of the boys shouting 'Look at the birds flying under that 'plane'. They weren't birds but bombs, and seconds later they exploded causing the biggest bangs we'd ever heard. My mother dashed out and shoved us one by one into an air-raid shelter father had constructed in the garden. We were packed in there like sardines, chattering excitedly and desperately anxious to get back outside to see what was going on!"

Cousins Mrs Joan Davey and Mrs Jean Parkinson of Pembroke Dock, were then schoolgirls playing in Sycamore Street, Bufferland. They have very good reason to vividly remember the appearance of the first Ju 88.

"It never entered our heads the aircraft was German", Mrs Davey admitted. "Indeed, to our delight the pilot and the man sitting next to him waved to us and we waved back most enthusiastically! Almost immediately afterwards there were some tremendous explosions, and the ground seemed to tremble".

The girls ran to the nearby home of Mrs Parkinson, who recalled "Inside our front door were stairs leading to the living room in the basement. As Joan and I dashed down, my mother and Gran were dashing up, and there was an almighty collision! But they were so relieved to see us that crashing into each other on the stairs didn't matter. Like Joan, I have always remembered those German airmen giving us a wave, and have wondered over the years whether they came through the war".

Eighteen year old John James was harvesting at West Pennar Farm for his uncle, Mr Tom Brace, and had an uninterrupted view of the Ju 88s diving in turn on the tanks before levelling out and climbing steeply over the haven.

He recalled "I had previously been watching a Walrus biplane lumber off the water. On a good day those old seaplanes could do 100 miles per hour and here was one, suddenly and almost certainly unwittingly, caught up in a deadly attack by three modern German bombers! If the situation hadn't been so terribly serious, it would have been laughable. As the third aircraft began to climb away from the tanks, it found the Walrus in its path and both had to bank sharply to avoid a head-on collision. What must the German airmen have thought when a tiny seaplane with a 'pusher' engine, and looking like a relic from the First World War, suddenly appeared right in front of them?"

John James then 18 – harvesting at West Pennar Farm when the first bombs fell. (*John James*)

The near collision obviously raised the hackles of the Walrus' two-man crew for according to Lord Parry of Neyland, then 14 years of age, the seaplane... "went raging after the Germans, gnashing its machine – gun like an old man's teeth, and showing the only defiance of an act of war in the high afternoon".

It was akin to a bicycle chasing a car.

Lord Parry, with schoolboy chums David Day and Freddie Griffiths, had been gathering blackberries on Barn Lake Bank, Neyland, when the German aircraft swooped. He remembered "The bomb noise was shattering, and through the black of the oil spume, flame climbed that was to roar and belch and burn for weeks".

(The Walrus spotted by Mr James and Lord Parry and his friends, almost certainly belonged to 764 Squadron, Fleet Air Arm, recently transferred

The schoolboy Gordon Parry – "flame climbed that was to roar and belch and burn for weeks".
(Lord Gordon Parry)

A formation of Walrus biplanes belonging to 764 Squadron, Fleet Air Arm, when based at Lawrenny Ferry later in the war. One of these veteran seaplanes almost collided with a Ju 88 when the raid was in progress.
(J. P. Issaverdens, via Ray Sturtivant)

Pembrokeshire's first civilian casualty of the war, Mr Fred Phillips of Pennar. He was thrashing corn in a field close to the tanks when the German bombers struck.

(Mrs Joyce Baldwin)

from a bomb-ravaged south coast base to what air and ground crew personnel had been assured would be "the much calmer waters of Pembroke Dock!")

Chaos prevailed in the upper area of Pembroke Dock. Shrieking mothers, some hysterical, were frantically looking for children, including a party of tots who'd gone blackberrying earlier in the afternoon in fields behind St Patrick's Church and less than half a mile from the oil tanks site. Scores of women and children were also blackberrying on the Barracks Hill, right next to the scene of the attack; theirs was a terrifying and shocking experience when the bombs exploded, yet miraculously no one was seriously hurt.

From the top of Military Road came a squealing noise which increased in intensity. Into view, and to add to the mayhem and confusion, ran some 50 terrified pigs from the piggery of local butcher George Burton, located near the tanks. The poor demented animals were coated with black, gluey oil. Some were blinded by the oil; several were literally on fire. It was hardly the most opportune time for the food-rationed population of Pennar to be offered roast pork on such a substantial scale. To add to the panic the smoke mass, gushing upwards in dense black clouds, began to obliterate the sun. At half past three on a lovely summer day, it was growing dark in Pembroke Dock by the minute.

Freshwater East sunbathers, and children and adults cooling off in the creamy surf, had a grandstand view of the Ju 88s – black crosses, glinting windows, pounding engines – as they sped past. Explosions followed a minute or so later, and smoke began to disfigure the skyline in the direction of Pembroke Dock.

Mrs Eva Phillips had already been warned the aircraft were German by Mr Courtney Price, occupant of the adjoining holiday bungalow, and a Royal Flying Corps veteran of the 1914-18 War. As soon as she saw the column of smoke, she guessed the tanks had been hit. She also realised that her husband and his brother had been threshing corn close by, and that she might already be a widow.

Fred Phillips heard the planes as they neared Pembroke Dock, but wasn't even given time to raise his head as he worked the horses in the sweltering mid-afternoon heat. Though a tall, heavily built man, the bomb blast lifted him completely off his feet and he was swept through the air before thumping painfully to the ground all of 50 yards away. As he lay there, semi-conscious and completely winded, a large stone blown free from earthworks around a tank, struck him painfully in the small of the back.

The Pennar farmer was stunned, bruised, bleeding and in considerable pain. But by the end of the day he had made a good recovery and was subsequently hailed in the press as "Pembroke Dock's first civilian casualty". As luck would have it, brother Ron was unharmed, but the panic -stricken horses broke free of their harness and another three weeks would pass before the last one was rounded up. Witnesses saw farm workers in an adjoining field have their shirts whipped off by blast when the first of the bombs made contact.

At her Beach Road home in Llanreath, Mrs Addie John was preparing her husband's tea when there was a thunderous explosion and part of the kitchen ceiling collapsed. Such is human nature that for a couple of seconds she showed more concern for her ruined apple dumplings than the dust and debris around her.

Upstairs in the front of the house Sid John woke with a start. There had been a bang of some sort, and he was puzzled why it was so dark. It wasn't like his wife to forget to call him. He reached for the clock, saw it was only sixteen minutes after three, and then padded across to the window. Tugging the curtains apart he looked out on a nightmare scene of smoke and flame, and heard cries and screams of terror as villagers grasped what had happened just across the narrow valley from their home.

Mrs Annie Munro had just finished pegging out a line of washing at 8 Beach Road, when the tank blew up. She reached the house seconds before the blast swept across the valley and then, with her mother, took shelter under the stairs. As they cowered there, neither could understand why there had been no air raid warning.

After shopping for her mother, May Tobin arrived back at Llanreath at exactly quarter past three. As she was about to insert the key in the lock of the front door the tank erupted and the blast blew her – and the door – right up the hallway of the family home in Orielton Terrace. The young girl was still deeply traumatised when arrangements were made for her and her mother and sister to be accommodated that night in St John's Vicarage.

Just inside the Military Road entrance to the tanks site was a house known as "Tank Villa." It was the home of Bill Ballard, storehouseman-in-charge of the oil tank depots at Pembroke Dock, his wife Winifred and daughter Maureen. The family had recently moved in following Bill's transfer from Sheerness Dockyard. He was offered the choice of going to Singapore or Pembroke Dock, and chose the latter on his wife's suggestion. She had said "Let's go to Wales; it'll be nice and quiet there!"

Maureen was playing in the garden with two newly found friends when the first bombs fell close by. Ironically, a workman had just finished digging an air raid shelter in a corner of the garden when the first Ju 88 roared overhead, no more than a couple of hundred feet high. He ushered the petrified girls, together with Mrs Ballard who'd emerged from the house fearing for their lives, to comparitive safety some 400 yards away from the site. Not long afterwards "Tank Villa" caught fire and was destroyed along with most of the family's belongings. Bill Ballard, in the dockyard when the German raiders struck, was soon reunited with his wife and daughter, overcome with relief to find them safe and well.

Gerald Donovan and Jim Griffiths, both of Pembroke Dock, were working in Number One Moat at the tanks complex. They saw the first aircraft approaching and black objects falling away from its bloated belly. The men fell flat on their faces and the ground shook violently as bombs exploded all around with a sharp CRUMPHH sound.

The one that found the target caused a shattering explosion and a wave of intense heat that seared through the moat. The two clambered out and ran for their lives to the 600 yards long underground tunnel which linked the tanks to the dockyard and served as an air raid shelter for Admiralty civilian personnel throughout the hostilities. There they met up with other breathless and badly shaken local workmen, including 29 year old Ivor James. He had been laying oil lines in the moat and said afterwards "Suddenly all hell broke loose."

The men re-mustered and, under the direction of Mr William Rees, Military Road, cautiously advanced with their own fire-fighting equipment in an effort to do what they could until the local brigades arrived. Gerald Donovan said later " It was a hopeless task – like peeing against the wind".

People living in the south-east of Pembroke thought the town's castle was on fire because the towering Norman fortress was in direct line with the Llanreath inferno. Incredibly, hundreds of Pembroke residents, less

1015
SE 217
OIL DUMP PEMBROKE DOCK 51°41'N. 04°57'W. 19.8.40.

This remarkable photograph was taken from an Avro Anson of 217 Squadron RAF Carew Cheriton, only a matter of minutes after the Ju 88s struck. The French oil tanker 'Franche Compte' can be seen preparing to leave stern first for Milford. The towering column of smoke has already cast a giant shadow across Pennar and Bufferland, part of the town of Pembroke Dock to the right, and much of the surrounding countryside. In the immediate foreground is the parish of Monkton, and Hundleton village is just out of the picture on the left. The bomb run took the enemy aircraft over Hundleton, Lower Pennar and Bufferland, seen sloping down to the Pembroke River in the middle of the photograph. The long line of houses leading up to the fire are in Military Road, where chaos was soon to reign. The hamlet of Llanreath is immediately behind the blaze. It is more than likely that when the RAF photographer took this picture, the German bombers were still flying down the haven, their crews congratulating themselves on a text-book operation. *(Public Record Office, Air 28/733)* than three miles away, didn't even hear the explosion and had no idea a major catastrophe had occurred.

At Humber's Bakery in Bridgend Terrace, Pembroke, 18 year old Gordon Griffiths of Monkton, and William Crawford, Tenby, knocked off work at twenty five past three. They stepped outside and the Tenby man, pointing upwards said "Look at that bloody great black cloud! It's going to rain buckets in a minute!" Raining it soon was, over Llanreath and Pennar, as a steady shower of minute oil drops poured down on the twin communities.

Betty Davies and Grace Griffiths were ordering ice cream in a Tenby cafe when the premises rocked and crockery and cutlery rattled. Someone said there was an explosion at sea, because that was where the boom had come from. But within minutes a woman entered the cafe to enthusiastically spread the news that German bombers were over Pembroke Dock and the town's Pennar district had been " flattened ". The Pennar girls fled, weeping and firmly believing they would never see their families again. They caught an early bus to Pembroke Dock and an enormous column of smoke in the sky did nothing to allay their fears.

An hour before the attack the French tanker *Franche Compte* left her Milford buoy for Pembroke Dockyard to top up with oil. She already had 11,000 tons on board. The tanker was in charge of the Dutch tug *Weichel* for'ard, and *Superman* – a Humber tug – aft. On the bridge with the French captain was Milford pilot Harry Fountain, and as the vessel straightened up alongside the dockyard jetty for mooring, the first stick of bombs exploded.

These are pilot Fountain's vivid recollections of the raid: "We saw a German bomber climb steeply right in front of us, leaving behind a blazing oil tank and a great cloud of smoke. Through the smoke came two more bombers and they also soared upwards. All three then made off down the haven on the southern side. The bombing happened very quickly and without warning; it was all over in a couple of minutes. The ship's master kept asking 'Why are no guns firing at the Germans?' I was more concerned with the tanks, which were right above the dockyard, and the awful thought of blazing oil cascading down on us. Grabbing a megaphone I shouted to the captain of *Superman* 'Tow away your end – and back to Milford!' Along with the Dutch tug we returned stern first, the French crew and the chaps on the tugs anxiously scanning the sky in case more Jerries were about. We were a sitting duck and, with all that oil on board, a well aimed German bomb would have blown us to kingdom come! Every ship we passed, large and small, had its crew crowded on deck, the men all staring as if hypnotised, at the blazing oil tank. Those vessels which were armed, had their guns manned, but by then it was too late. The birds had flown".

When the telephone rang at Pembroke Dock fire brigade headquarters at twenty past three, Chief Morris and Section Leader Harry Baker didn't need to be told what the message was. Baker was screaming blue murder because the siren hadn't sounded, and he bawled "If the ARP let the public down like this again, there'll be no messing about. I'll sound the bloody thing myself!"

Firemen, nearly all of them part-timers, were arriving at the Market House in a steady stream – "like a lot of excited schoolkids", someone would remember later. This was what they'd volunteered for; this was what they'd trained for. This was the "Big One". They were confident they could cope.

At half past three, in a couple of Merryweather fire engines and a convoy of support vehicles, the Pembroke Dock fire brigade charged bravely up to Pennar. Only Chief Arthur Morris was experienced enough to know he and his gallant men were charging into the very jaws of hell.

The main strength of the council-operated Pembroke Dock and Pembroke fire brigades, along with others in Pembrokeshire, was provided by auxiliaries, better known as retained men or part – timers. If they didn't happen to be at the fire station when an emergency arose, they had to report there as soon as they could, sometimes from the most inconvenient locations.

Alf Grieve was lucky. He was chatting with local contractor Stanley Jones in Front Street yard, only a couple of minutes sprinting distance from the Pembroke Dock brigade headquarters, when the tank exploded. Grieve had already begun running along Front Street as the first of the Ju 88s rapidly gained height following its attack.

Within 15 minutes he was kitted up and at the steering wheel of a fire engine with Chief Morris alongside him. In the back were Deputy Chief Arthur Skone, and Firemen Joe John, Fred Sillence, Charlie Emment, Billy McMurren, Billy Lloyd and Jim Poldo. These men would be the very first fire brigade personnel to arrive at the Llanreath inferno. Nearly 15 minutes had elapsed since the bombing and the German planes were on their way "home".

Pembroke Dock engine fitter Bert Mathias, working on a merchantman lying off Milford, watched them clear the haven's entrance at about 2,000 feet. So did several hundred people in Milford's new open-air swimming pool on the sea-front. Yet it was not until half past three that the air raid siren wailed out its warning in Pembroke Dock!

Fireman Grieve was a first class driver but had to summon all his skill and experience to manoeuvre the fire engine up Military Road. The street, one of the longest and widest in South Pembrokeshire, was crowded with people, most of whom appeared to be running in no particular direction. Many of the women were weeping, others looking dazed and confused. Scampering pigs, squealing loudly, were being driven down the road from the piggery at the other end.

After forcing a passage up the street, the firemen drew closer to the tanks complex. Jet black smoke was churning across the carriageway in such dense clouds it was impossible for them to see. But they were aware that in there somewhere Admiralty workmen, using Beresford pumps, were battling heroically against the flames. Alf Grieve would recall later "If there is such a thing as motoring into hell, that's what we did. We were completely blind and only found the turn-off into the tanks depot by pure luck."

* ·⚬⚬⚬· *

The first Ju 88 had scored a direct hit on a tank containing 12, 000 gallons of oil, and the sheer size and intensity of the fire stunned the men. It was an awesome sight. The blaze was creating a deafening roaring noise and as the brigade personnel stood there, shielding their faces from the scorching heat, Chief Morris bellowing to

The Junkers 88, which formed the backbone of the German bomber force. It could carry a bomb load of up to 5,500 pounds and when war broke out was regarded, in terms of performance and versatility, as the finest bomber aircraft in service with any air force in the world. *(John Worley Collection)*

make himself heard, said "We need everybody up here – where the hell are they?"

His deputy, Arthur Skone, yelled back "If they're having as much bloody trouble finding the entrance to this place as we did, they might not get here at all".

The Chief retorted "God forbid…" He was worried, deeply worried. And for personal reasons as well. His own home was at 23 Military Road. His invalid wife, confined to a wheelchair, and 12 year old daughter Pat, were there. He knew that if the inferno got out of control, if it spread to other tanks, the entire street could be incinerated – perhaps the whole of Pennar. Whether they wanted to or not, people would have to be evacuated, especially those whose homes were nearest the tanks.

⁘ ⁙⦿⦾⦿⁙ ⁘

At the Pembroke brigade headquarters by the Town Hall, there was confusion for some time over where the fire actually was. A report came through that Priory Farm, Monkton, home of local personality and councillor, George Jenkins, was alight and the duty crew sped over there, convinced by the volume of smoke rising from that direction that they would find the place razed to the ground.

Regular fireman Eddie Jones had already guessed the tanks had been hit. But until this was officially confirmed the retained men and off – duty regulars, by then arriving in large numbers, would have to stay put. Jones, together with firemen Sid Williams and Tom Lewis, had seen the planes pass over from the south but had not positively identified them as hostile.

Then a vivid orange flash raked the sky behind the castle. Even on a bright, sunny afternoon, it was dazzling. A very loud explosion followed seconds later. When the message finally came through shortly after 3. 30pm, 29 year old Jones didn't waste a second. Slamming down the phone he raced from the office and bawled to knots of waiting firemen "It's the tanks! We're on our way, let's go!"

Among his crew was Pembroke cinema proprietor Len Haggar. As the fire engine nosed out into Main Street watched by a large and anxious crowd, he spotted a man gesticulating wildly. It was the cinema's head projectionist, Harold Smith.

"He was dancing about like a madman", Haggar would remember afterwards. "He kept shouting that if he didn't have the bloody keys to the bloody cinema there wouldn't be any bloody pictures that night! I tossed him the keys from the moving fire engine; he caught them, grinned and gave the thumbs up sign. It was just as well he remembered the keys because the way it turned out I wouldn't enter my cinema again for another three weeks."

When they got to Military Road the Pembroke personnel ran into the same mayhem in the smoke-shrouded street that firemen from all over Pembrokeshire would encounter late that afternoon and in the evening. They would remember an elderly woman standing on a pavement, wearing a dressing gown and carpet slippers. She was sobbing bitterly and every now and then shouted at passing firemen "For Christ's sake get us out of here! Get us out – will you!

Two other Pembroke part-timers, taxi operator Ron Campbell and Billy Neil, licensee of the Waterman's Arms, left at different times for Pennar in their own cars to link up with brigade colleagues already there. By then smoke from the stricken tank was drifting low over the area like enormous puffs of black cotton wool. Conditions were so appalling that when Campbell arrived in Military Road he couldn't see the bonnet of the car. Clutching a handkerchief to his face as the choking smoke seeped into the vehicle, he made slow progress up the road by keeping the front and rear wheels in the gutter and in contact with the kerb. He reached the end of the street after a nightmare car crawl to be confronted by the ultimate horror – the blazing tank.

Coal merchants Lawford and Freddie Morgan heard the bang and saw the smoke while loading their lorry in the coalyard at Pembroke Dock railway station. The brothers were both auxiliaries and after heaving the bulging sacks off the lorry, reported for duty at the Market House. There a very dirty, dusty coal vehicle was requisitioned for brigade use by Section Leader Harry Baker. The Morgans then set off for the tanks, stopping for retained fireman Charles Thomas as he hurried on foot towards Pennar.

Thirty two year old Sid Hay, with his nephew, Billy, was delivering goods to houses in the village of Carew when the Ju 88s struck. Leaving his young relative to complete the round Hay, a well known rugby forward who had played for Llanelli, hoisted his burly frame on to the running board of a passing beer wagon and instructed the startled drayman to "drive like the clappers to Pembroke Dock!" Five miles and 15 minutes later the part-time fireman signed in at brigade headquarters.

On the other side of the haven Jack Vincent, aged 35, had been trying to persuade the housewives of Burton village to buy the latest Singer sewing machine since half past nine that morning. He'd enlisted as an auxiliary with the Pembroke Dock brigade three months previously and was still impatiently waiting to attend something bigger than a chimney fire. When the tank erupted in an orange glow and what looked like black velvet shot into the sky, the dapper salesman couldn't believe his eyes. This was what he'd been waiting for. Accelerating his Austin 7 to the limit in a hectic dash to Neyland pontoon, he got there to discover that the crew of the ferry boat were refusing to take it over to Pembroke Dock in case "Jerry was still hanging about".

He fretted and fumed for three quarters of an hour before the ferry skipper reluctantly conceded it was probably safe to cast off. Jack Vincent stood on the deck beside his Austin 7 as the vessel made its passage to Pembroke Dock, thinking naively "I hope the lads keep the fire going until I get there!"

Thirty year old retained fireman George Fish, also a part-time postman, was delivering letters at the top end of Military Road when he saw the first Junkers shed its load. He watched fascinated as the bombs appeared to drop straight initially before sloping off towards the tanks. As they exploded in rapid succession, one finding the target with a tremendous bang, George Fish played it according to the book. He had a double responsibility – to the post office and the fire service.

Though closer to the enemy's objective than any other fireman that fateful afternoon, he decided to dash to a sub-post office in close proximity, drop off his postbag, and then run hell for leather to the fire station, about a mile away. He arrived there almost the same time as auxiliary fireman Bill Griffiths, who'd been sunning himself in the garden of his home in Ferry Road, Lower Pennar, when the attack occurred. Griffiths had grabbed a rickety bicycle belonging to a neighbour and pedalled off furiously to report for duty. As both men checked in along with others, the first fire engine, with Chief Arthur Morris urging driver Grieve to make all haste, was about to leave for Pennar.

· ·⊹·⊱◦⊰·⊹· ·

Mrs Eva Phillips came home on the first available transport from Freshwater East to find her husband Fred shocked and bruised, but otherwise all right after his traumatic experience. Betty Davies and Grace Griffiths arrived from Tenby shortly afterwards to find, with overwhelming relief, that Pennar was still standing but very much in turmoil.

A number of families in Military Road and nearby Owen Street were preparing to move out before nightfall, including Betty's parents, Mr and Mrs W. G. Davies, who had arranged to stay with relatives in Jeffreyston, a village some miles away. As an ambulance driver, their daughter would have to remain in Pennar on standby. Her uncle, Charles Davies, who shared the family home at Southside, Military Road, would keep her company.

Throughout the late afternoon there was a steady exodus from Llanreath and by the evening it had become a ghost village. Residents, some in a state of deep shock, had scattered taking refuge where they could and carrying only essential belongings. Mrs Munro and her mother had left, May Tobin and her mother and sister were being cared for in St John's Vicarage (why the family was sent there has not been established), and Mrs Addie John went to her step-mother's home in Pembroke Dock. She spent that night in the cellar of the house with her infant daughter. Her husband Sid, who had belonged to the pre-war Pembroke Dock fire brigade, reported for night-shift work at Milford Armament Depot on time, but was then instructed to return to Pembroke Dock to take charge

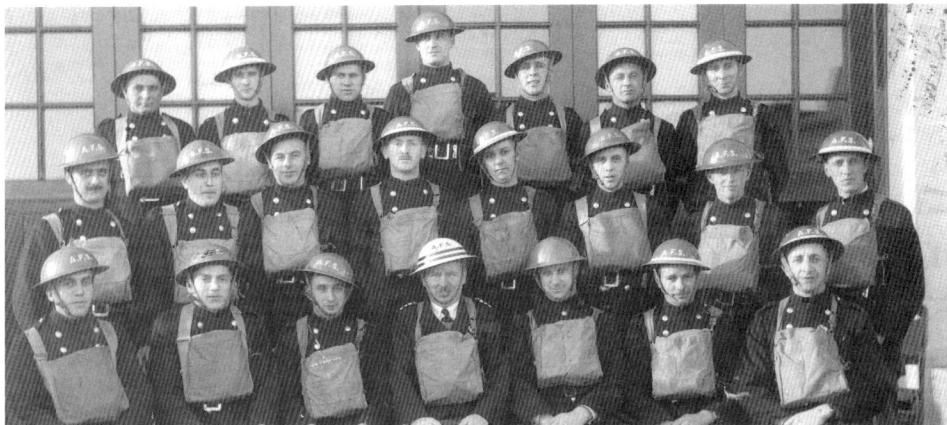

Members of Milford Haven Fire Brigade photographed in the summer of 1940. Seated centre wearing a white helmet is Brigade Commandant Horace Howarth, and to his left is Chief Matt Acornley. Others identified, all left to right, are back: Harry Jones, Herbert Jones, Dick Yolland, Cecil Foster, Frank John, ?, Thompson; middle: Hands, Chris Darlington, Stockwood Rees, ?, Eddie Gough, Jim Evans, ?, Jones; front: Ted Evans, Cole, Cyril John, Horace Howarth, Matt Acornley, Harry Byard, Leo Jones. This is not a full complement of Milford firemen because the total strength of the brigade was then around 32. (Raymond Evans)

of the Admiralty fire engine there. So urgent was the requirement for men with fire service experience that a navy launch was provided to take him to the upper reaches of the haven where he disembarked at the dockyard's Carr Jetty. Some Llanreath families cleared off so quickly and in such panic after the German raid that they left their homes unlocked. At nightfall armed soldiers were patrolling the village as a precaution against looters.

By then brigades from all over Pembrokeshire were at the scene of the inferno. Chief Morris had demanded reinforcements and was getting them. Civilian and military police from over a wide area were also sent to Pennar to keep the route to the tanks clear as support brigades poured in.

Tenby left at 4.39pm, Narberth at 4.40, and Haverfordwest 4.53. At 6.13 the small Neyland contingent of firemen requested and received permission to cross the haven to assist their Pembroke Dock and Pembroke colleagues. Fishguard departed at 6.37 and eight minutes later came the very heartening news that Swansea, under the command of Chief Alec Davies, was sending assistance. The Carmarthen fire engine moved off at 6.56. A trailer pump belonging to this brigade actually left at 5.12 but broke down soon afterwards. It had still not been repaired by midnight.

Questions would later be raised about the failure of the Milford Haven brigade to lend weight sooner than it did. Thirty six year old full-time fireman Harry Jones cycled to the brigade's headquarters behind the Town Hall after seeing the towering column of smoke over Pembroke Dock.

Waiting there was Matt Acornley, a Lancastrian who'd been appointed Milford's fire chief the previous January. He appeared agitated and snapped at arriving firemen "The tanks have been bombed. Get your gear on – we're going over !"

Jones, who drove the Leyland fire engine, jumped into the cab and George Forrest, Alan Murray, Jimmy Britton and Sidney John among others, clambered into the back.

"Chief Acornley then went into the office, leaving us ready to go and raring to go", Jones recalled in later years. "We waited for a quarter of an hour and then the Chief came out saying 'It's all right lads – our assistance is not required'. We climbed out and stood around feeling completely deflated. I slipped across the road to the sea-front and could see a huge fire was raging at Pembroke Dock. I ran back to report and as I got to the office the telephone rang. Then the Chief hurried out and said "Right! We're going this time!"

That afternoon proved a jittery one for lots of people. When the Milford fire engine was en-route to Neyland ferry pontoon, driver Jones saw a twin-engined aircraft, which he and Matt Acornley took to be hostile, coming in their direction. Jones stopped, yelled "Take cover!" and the firemen leapt out, some crouching in a hedgerow, others slithering under their vehicle. Seconds later they sheepishly emerged, after the plane had roared over displaying RAF roundels. It was an Avro Anson!

The Milford brigade experienced more frustrating delay at Neyland because at first the ferry boat's crew thought the Leyland was too large and cumbersome to be accommodated on board. It was eventually reversed on to the vessel, which made a special trip across. By then the Milford men were very angry they hadn't left for Pembroke Dock earlier to assist their south county colleagues. When they did get there, over one and a half hours had passed since Chief Acornley had originally ordered them to move off.

For some reason, which was never subsequently explained, while the departure to Pembroke Dock of every other Pembrokeshire brigade was recorded in the Milford brigade log book for Monday afternoon and evening, August 19th 1940, no mention was made of when their own men left. In fact, no mention was made that they left at all.

Chief Acornley never explained who it was telephoned to say that Milford's assistance was not required when, in the words of Harry Jones, the men were ready and raring to go help fight a fire which, even at that stage, was of disasterous proportions. Certainly, no such message was sent by the Pembroke Dock brigade who were phoning around for all the assistance and support they could get. It seemed an insignificant matter at the time. Some months later however, certain people would have reason to remember it – and wonder.

But on that evening of August 19th, with smoke engulfing Pennar, Pembroke Dock's fire chief didn't give a damn that the Milford contingent had showed up late. He was only too pleased to see them. Firemen were faced with the awesome responsibility of saving a whole community from death and destruction.

It was going to be a long and demanding night.

• ⋅⋅⋅:●⊃●⊂●⊱═⋅⋅ •   ⸺

In the late afternoon and early evening of that Monday, a number of firemen reported seeing a small boy inside the oil tanks site.

Harry Jones of the Milford brigade recalled "When I first spotted him he was not too far away from the burning tank, and I saw him twice after that. He couldn't have been more than 10, but things were so hectic and we were so busy there was no opportunity to ask him who he was, and what he was doing in such a dangerous place".

For 40 years the identity of this lad remained a mystery but then, in 1980, on the 40th anniversary of the oil tanks raid, the *Western Telegraph* received a letter from Mr G. L. Lowther, Greenhill Crescent, Merlins Bridge, Haverfordwest. He wrote that on the day the tanks were bombed he was an 11 year old from Narberth who had spent the morning at the Pembroke Mart ground with his uncle.

The letter went on "Early in the afternoon we were passing Pembroke Castle when we heard an explosion from the direction of Pembroke Dock. Within seconds thick clouds of black smoke rose into the atmosphere and we realised that the oil tanks at Llanreath had been hit.

"My uncle, a senior member of Narberth fire brigade, immediately got on the 'phone to inform them about the bombing. We then rushed over to Llanreath in uncle's van and were allowed to stay there until the brigade arrived from Narberth. Very soon fire engines from all over the county were there.

"It certainly was an experience for an 11 year old. I think I must have stayed among the firemen for at least three hours watching them perform the hopeless task of trying to extinguish the fire. No one seemed to mind the presence of a young lad. Looking back it seems an irresponsible action on the part of my uncle to have exposed me to so much danger. But on the other hand he could not have left me in the town on my own without some fear of the German bombers returning and causing further damage. I was eventually taken back to Narberth in a car driven by a friend of my uncle. My grand-parents, with whom I was spending part of the summer holiday, were very worried and concerned about my welfare and were glad to see I was safe and sound".

CHAPTER FIVE

AUGUST 19TH – 23RD

In the line of duty

We all knew Chief Morris had been given a wage increase. It was reported in the local press. When we got to the fire I heard him say to his deputy
"My God! I'm paying a terrible price for that ten bob rise!..."

Fireman Tommy Gibby, Pembroke Dock.

Work on the construction of the Admiralty oil tanks had started in 1925 and when completed the depot – situated on a promontory high above Pembroke Dock, and very close to Llanreath and Pennar – accommodated a total of 17 tanks.

Each tank, about 100 feet in diameter, stood in a saucer-like depression so that any overflow could be contained, and the Admiralty eventually decided to link these depressions to a huge moat. Curling around treble rows of tanks in a crescent shape, the moat had only been partially completed by August 1940 and men like Gerald Donovan, Jim Griffiths and Ivor James, were working on the extension when they spotted the Ju 88s coming in from the south-east.

Ten years earlier the RAF had established a flying boat base at Pembroke Dock, and airmen had immediately noticed how vulnerable the tanks would be to aerial assault if Britain became involved in another major war. This point was brought to the attention of the Air Ministry who, in turn, alerted the Admiralty. But nothing was done until the uneasy spring of 1939 when plans were drawn up for the moat's construction. Work got under way in June, three months before the outbreak of war. The moat was approximately 1,500 feet long, 400 feet wide and 40 feet deep It was designed to prevent oil flowing across and out of the depot should the tanks be pierced in an air raid.

As he grimly surveyed the fire shortly before midnight on Monday August 19th, Chief Arthur Morris consoled himself with the thought that if luck wasn't on the firefighters' side during the hours ahead, if the tank was to boil over and the burning oil spread, the moat, even in its unfinished state, would allow his men precious seconds, perhaps even minutes, to flee to safety.

By then he'd had time to assess the immediate situation and was reasonably confident that with some 80 Pembrokeshire firemen on hand, plus a very dependable bunch of Admiralty workmen who'd been at the scene longer than anyone, the blaze could be confined to the violated tank, at least until further reinforcements from South Wales arrived.

So far the measures taken had been simple enough and effective enough. To prevent the blaze from escalating and endangering life and property in Pennar and Llanreath, the burning tank had been isolated and the others kept cool by a constant curtain of water provided by all the jets that could be mustered. There had been anxiety earlier on when, because of pipe corrosion, the pressure from the town mains had gradually reduced to a trickle. But this was soon rectified by what then appeared to be an unlimited supply of sea water from nearby Llanreath beach.

Chief Morris was also aware that two of the 17 tanks didn't contain oil. They were filled with water as a form of insurance against the very sort of emergency now confronting the firemen. As he strode to and fro bellowing encouragement to the men, Morris spotted his Milford counterpart Matt

"Smoke from the fire could be seen as far away as Somerset." This photograph, taken from Neyland, is of special interest to aviation enthusiasts because of two aircraft to be seen on the right. Immediately in front of the dockyard sheerlegs is a Short Brothers 'Empire' civilian flying-boat, and close by is a Swordfish floatplane. (Pembrokeshire Records Office ref HDX/101/64)

Acornley, and shouted "We just might win this, but we've got to keep the water flowing". Acornley, who'd been staggered by the size of the fire, yelled back "I think we're going to beat it".

By 11pm scores of families who had evacuated their homes were bedding down in the open on the Barracks Hill because they had nowhere else to go. Others, more fortunate, were billeted with relatives and friends in the lower area of Pembroke Dock, in neighbouring Pembroke, and surrounding villages and hamlets.

One of the last to leave Llanreath was 30 year old Mrs Alice Goodrick, Hill House, Beach Road. Her husband Robert, a survivor of the retreat to Dunkirk, had only returned to his unit a few days earlier after spending a week's leave at home. She would recall "Nobody wanted to go that night, and I stayed longer than most. But every time the tank flared with an awful growling noise, our home vibrated violently. It was like being in a house of cards, waiting for it to fall apart. With my two daughters, Ena, who was nine, and baby Pamela, I left for Pembroke. As I closed the front door after me I noticed that all the paint was peeling off."

Inhabitants of Pembroke Dock and the neighbouring waterfront communities of Neyland and Milford Haven would spend an anxious, restless night. Many would remember it as the longest night of their lives. They were only too well aware that if the Luftwaffe came back, the three towns and adjacent military targets would look as prominent from the air as if it was daylight, because the brilliant glow cast by the enormous fire was making a mockery of the blackout precautions.

In Pembroke Dock there was considerable bitterness and resentment over the fact three enemy aircraft had been allowed to fly in, drop their bombs, and fly out again without as much as a rifle being fired at them. To add considerable insult to injury, the air raid siren had not sounded until the Germans had gone !

• ·:·=｛●ᗪ⊗ᗤ●｝=·:· •

Things went dramatically wrong for the firefighters an hour before daybreak on Tuesday August 20th. Suddenly the water pressure slackened until scarcely a dribble was coming through. Firemen who had stood for hours like robots, forming a disciplined curtain of water with their jets, slouched forward as the pressure ceased. For many it was the first relaxed stance they had assumed since the previous afternoon and evening.

What had gone wrong? Everyone wanted to know. The answer was not long coming. A message was relayed from Llanreath beach. There was no more water because the tide had gone out! For a couple of minutes Morris was too stunned to react. Then, pulling himself together, he began barking orders. A general alarm would have to be issued; there was no alternative. Additional men, plus a lot more equipment, would be urgently needed because there was now a real danger of the entire oil fuel depot going up in flames.

As Arthur Morris quickly called a conference with the chiefs of other brigades, he knew he would soon be relinquishing command. Top brass would be taking over.

At dawn firemen, aching in every limb, blackened faces caked with grime, were getting the last of six fire engines back up on to firm and reasonably flat ground at the top of Llanreath beach. They'd followed the tide out as far as they could and then had to halt. A few more yards and their appliances would have become bogged down in a deep layer of clinging mud.

Later regular fireman Eddie Jones of Pembroke, would recall "When we lost the sea water we lost a crucial battle. If we could have continued pumping water up Llanreath hill that particular morning, there might have been a completely different story to tell about the oil tanks fire, and the lives of firemen might have been saved. As it was, we were beaten by the tide".

The tanks bombing made Pembroke Borough Council realise the importance of having additional permanent firemen in their two brigades. This photograph, taken in late September 1940, shows members of Pembroke Dock's "Red Shift" after they had become full-time firemen. They are pictured with Chief Arthur Morris (far right). Left to right are: Harry Baker, "Tot" Davies, Ivor Jenkins, George Fish, Billy Jones, Alf Dooley, Jack Treadwell, Bob Etherington and Tommy Gibby. The last named became a senior staff officer in the West Riding of Yorkshire Fire Service after the war, before retiring to Lamphey, Pembroke.

(Author's Collection)

At 8am on Tuesday August 20th, Captain Tom Breaks, Chief Inspector of the Fire Brigades Division at the Home Office, received a priority telephone call.

He was told the situation was worsening at Pembroke Dock, and there were real fears the major fire there might get completely out of control. Would he go to the scene and take charge? He was promised as many men as he required, providing they weren't drawn from areas where German bombing was severe.

Breaks finished his breakfast and got in touch with the Paddington booking office to make sure a reserved seat would be available on the night train to Pembroke Dock. He also began an extensive check to establish which of the larger English brigades were able to spare men for the West Wales fire.

Three hours later Mrs Phyllis Hammond, Superintendent of the St John Ambulance Division at Pembroke Dock, and Mrs Greathead, Commandant of the Pembroke Red Cross Detachment, were advised by telephone that there would be a major build-up of firemen at Pembroke Dock before the end of the week. The caller disclosed that the men would be billeted in Pennar School, and the Temperance Hall in Pembroke Dock town centre, and that a casualty station was to be set up in St Patrick's church hall, Pennar, which was conveniently close to the fire. It would be greatly appreciated if the St John Ambulance Division and the Red Cross Detachment could be in a full state of readiness by that evening.

At mid-day on the 20th a second tank caught fire. By then an adequate water supply from the old "pickling pond" in the dockyard (a relic from the days when Pembroke Dock was one of Britain's biggest and most successful ship-building yards), and Pennar Gut, had been restored to the depot. Fire floats and a boom defence barge carrying pumping units were also being manoeuvred into position at deep water mark off Llanreath beach. But the time lapse when no water was available had taken its toll. What everybody feared had happened. Another tank was ablaze.

For miles around the fire was presenting a sombre and awe-inspiring spectacle. The column of smoke was some 400 to 500 feet across, over 1,000 feet high, and spreading out over South Pembrokeshire and the open sea in a south-easterly direction as far as the eye could see. It had already been reported that the smoke could be seen in Somerset.

As they fought the flames many of the firemen were cloaked in a thick pall of choking smoke, and despite constant use of lime and chalk to mark the roads, it was impossible for vehicles, even with full headlights, to move at more than walking pace. The din from the inferno was another hazard. It prevented drivers from hearing the approach of other vehicles and as they couldn't see in the first place, there were a number of collisions and numerous near misses. Every so often the suffocating heat became unbearable as the burning tanks erupted, spouting great tongues of flame which created an incandescent mass above them.

Throughout the first full day Pembrokeshire firemen and contingents from Carmarthen and Swansea, courageously held their ground against the most frightening and vicious fire of its kind Britain had ever known. They were filthy dirty, dog-tired, very hungry and, in the furnace-like heat, constantly thirsty. They were definitely not in the mood for the sort of bizarre situation in which 10 Milford firemen found themselves involved very early on the morning of Wednesday August 21st.

After being relieved the men were travelling home in a truck towing a trailer. At the wheel was auxiliary fireman Jack Philpin, aged 31, with Chief Acornley in the passenger seat. As the vehicle clattered along Slebech Flats, near Haverfordwest, at 1.14 am, several shots rang out and it was struck by bullets.

"We pulled up, got out, and found ourselves surrounded by uniformed Home Guardsmen, some of whom were armed with rifles and flashing torches," Philpin would remember. "They said they were operating a road block and that we should have stopped. The truth was we were so tired we didn't even see them, and because of the blackout it was pitch dark. The Chief was livid. He said something like 'How the hell are we going to win this war with stupid bastards like you lot on our side!' The experience shook us. To think we could have been killed by the Home Guard! I must admit, however, our appearance was most undesirable and at a time when there were supposed to be spies about, we looked anything but firemen, especially by torch-light!"

There had also been a case of mistaken identity the previous afternoon when a Blenheim from 236 Squadron, RAF St Eval, Cornwall, was actually damaged by ship-borne gun fire as it flew over Pembroke Dock. The aircraft managed to limp back to base, its crew, Pilot Officer G.L. Campbell and Sergeant S. Archer, anxiously searching the sky for signs of the real enemy!

While the Milford firemen were being "ambushed" at Slebech Flats, ten Cardiff pumps with their crews were leaving for Pembroke Dock in command of Superintendent Bainbridge of the City of Cardiff Brigade. They left behind a number of personnel including 30 year old regular fireman Stanley Israel. These men were bitterly disappointed they had been denied the opportunity of fighting a "real fire" at Pembroke Dock.

A few minutes before 7am on Wednesday August 21st, the overnight train from London pulled into Pembroke Dock station and among the many people who stepped out on to the platform amid a cloud of hissing steam, was an enigmatic figure who was to play a key and controversial role in the battle to quell the oil tanks fire.

Captain Tom Breaks was met by auxiliary firemen Alf Grieve who

Pembroke Dock firemen Billy Russan, Jack Vincent, Freddie Devonald, Frankie Nicholas, Sid Phillips and Alf Grieve pose with the tail fin of a German bomb which fell wide of the Llanreath depot and failed to explode. Alf Grieve, standing right, drove the first fire engine to arrive at the inferno, and was the fireman detailed to meet Captain Thomas Breaks when he arrived in Pembroke Dock from London. (Author's Collection)

saluted smartly and then drove the distinguished arrival straight to Pennar. Breaks was visibly shaken when he saw the dense smoke they had to drive through in order to get to the depot's pumping station, and kept exclaiming "Good God!" The man from the Home Office set up his quarters at the pumping station and, as he unpacked, watched recently arrived Cardiff firemen filing in orderly fashion up to where the tanks were blazing.

At 10am Breaks asked fireman Grieve to show him the burning tanks at close quarters. The two men had climbed the steep bunding around the tanks to obtain a fuller view when suddenly – and dramatically – a twin-engined enemy aircraft came in low through the smoke. The plane caught the firefighters completely off guard because the roar of its engines had been deadened by the noise of the fire. Men ran in every direction searching for cover as the German aircraft made several low sweeps over the depot with guns blazing.

"Captain Breaks and I slid back swiftly to lower ground where we found a sheet of corrugated iron for protection – or what we thought was protection, because afterwards we found a similar sheet riddled with bullet holes", Grieve would recall. The two made a stooping dash to the underground tunnel where Breaks, after regaining his breath, jocularly told scores of sheltering firemen "The Jerries must have known I was coming!"

Most of the men had no idea who he was – it was hardly the most opportune time for introductions! – and anyway, they were in no mood for jokes. The appearance of the German plane had shaken them. It was bad enough having to fight a fire that had now reached massive proportions; being machine-gunned from the air was an additional hazard they could do without.

Breaks had been in Pembroke Dock for less than four hours, but already he was acutely aware of the frightful problems facing the firemen. He had originally estimated that between three and four hundred men would be sufficient to prevent the blaze from engulfing the entire depot. Now he estimated a couple of hundred more would have to be brought in without delay. And they were certainly going to need protection from marauding German aircraft.

At Cardiff fire brigade headquarters that afternoon an order was received that a six strong reinforcement party led by regular firemen Stanley Israel and Tommy Thomas, was to leave for Pembroke Dock in a Morris tender.

"Our spirits soared", Israel recalled. "We were going to link up with Superintendent Bainbridge and the other Cardiff personnel, to help fight the biggest blaze the brigade had been involved with up to then".

On the following day the inferno claimed five victims, killed in the line of duty. Heat had caused the metal wall of one of the burning tanks to buckle and burst open with a gigantic spurt of flame which completely

Thirty year old John Frederick Thomas, one of five Cardiff firemen who perished when they were enveloped by flame. (Mrs Violet Sellers)

enveloped five Cardiff firemen: Frederick George Davis, aged 31, 6 Llanbradach Street; Clifford Miles, also 31, 118 Brunswick Street, Canton; Ivor John Kilby, aged 29, 44 Gelligaer Street; Trevor Charles Morgan, aged 31, 46 Mey Street; and John Frederick Thomas, aged 30 of Elaine Street. Mills was the son of Jack Mills, a well known Welsh Rugby Union referee of that time.

Twenty six year old Iris Davis was at the hairdresser when told that her husband Fred had perished in the fire. In a state of shock she was taken home to her three young daughters, six year old twins June and Jean, and Edna, who was eight.

June, later Mrs Parle of Cardiff, recalled "Mum refused to accept that Dad was dead; that he wouldn't come home anymore. He had left for Pembroke Dock only the previous day, excited and as pleased as punch that he and the other boys were joining the city brigade's main force".

Devon-born Fred Davis was an upholsterer known throughout the Cardiff brigade as "Biddie", because he hailed from Bideford. Three more of the victims had also arrived in Pembroke Dock the day before. The other was a member of the original Cardiff party sent to the dockyard town.

In a report to the Pembrokeshire coroner at the inquest on August 30th, Captain Breaks said that around 1.15 on the afternoon in question,

Firemen and local councillors led by the Mayor, Councillor John Gwyther, follow the funeral cortege of the five Cardiff firemen. They are seen walking down from the Pembroke Dock mortuary, then in Upper Park Street. *(Mrs Betty Lomas)*

he was on a mound between two tanks and about 20 feet in front were five AFS men working one jet on a single tank. He did not know their identity as they wore oilskin clothing.

"A large burst of flame seemed to come from one of the tanks which appeared to envelope the men", Breaks continued. "I shouted, and they shouted, and we all made one stampede for safety. I was about 20 feet away and felt the blaze, but the reason I got away was that I am used to this sort of thing, and had start. The wind was blowing a gale at the time. The last I saw of the men they were running away from the fire".

The Coroner: Had you any idea this tank was going to burst?

Witness: It was absolutely unexpected. It is part of my duty to make sure men do not go into danger.

Replying to a further question, he said the theory was that the tank got so hot that the metal became soft and a big spurt of oil must have come out. It was quite reasonable to expect the Cardiff firemen to be working where they were, and there was no undue risk.

He added "While I am not attempting to evade any responsibility, I would like to say these men were most probably placed there by another officer, and might have been visited several times in the meantime. It was the concerted opinion there was no undue risk. In a fire of this sort it is never known when terrible dangers might occur to any men at one spot".

The Coroner returned a verdict that death was due to asphyxia and burning, accidentally caused. He observed "It is clear the men were carrying out normal duties at a dangerous fire. At such a fire an accident as described can occur unexpectedly and inexplicably. The nation owes these brave men a debt of gratitude".

He expressed sympathy with the bereaved relatives.

The Chief Constable of Cardiff, Mr J. A. Wilson, said he found no fault with the dispositions of the men at their posts. It was an unfortunate accident which could not have been forseen by anyone. The risks to firemen were immense, and he thought that the courage with which they carried out their duties was not fully appreciated by the general public. He expressed the Cardiff firemen's deep appreciation to the people of Pembroke Dock for the great kindnesses which had been shown them.

Fireman Jack Vincent of Pembroke Dock, who had been working close to where the men perished, was not called to give evidence at the inquest but had this to say later "Lots of us started running when flame shot out from the tank without warning. The trouble was the Cardiff men ran the wrong way; I saw the flame wrap itself around them. Chief Morris and I threw markers so they would know where to look for the bodies."

On the following Sunday St Patrick's Church, Pennar, was filled to capacity for a memorial service conducted by the Priest-in-Charge, the Rev John Theodore Morgan.

The firemen's remains were conveyed back to Cardiff for burial, and the *Telegraph* described the scene as the coffins were removed from the Pembroke Dock mortuary:

They were carried on a grey ARP ambulance car, and the streets were thronged with sympathisers and representatives of public services. Here and there was a splash

---

TEL.NO 7940.

IN YOUR REPLY
PLEASE QUOTE

TC/DD

CITY HALL,
CARDIFF.

19th September 1940

D. KENVYN REES.
TOWN CLERK.
CLERK OF THE PEACE

Dear Madam,

    At the last meeting of the City Council the Lord Mayor referred to the men of the Cardiff Auxiliary Fire Service who lost their lives whilst rendering assistance at a fire in West Wales on the 20th August last, and the following resolution was passed:-

    (1) That the Council place on record the names of Frederick George Davies, 6 Llanbradach Street; Ivor John Kilby, 44 Gelligaer Street; Trevor Charles Morgan, 46 May Street; John F. Thomas, 16 Elaine Street; and Clifford Mills, 188 Brunswick Street; who died doing their duty as bravely as if on the battlefield.
    (2) That an expression of sympathy be conveyed to their relatives."

    I desire personally to tender to you and your family my sincere condolence and my admiration of the devotion to duty of those who lost their lives on such a hazardous and dangerous task.

          Yours faithfully,

The letter sent by Cardiff City Council to the widows of the Cardiff firemen killed at Pembroke Dock.

of khaki, and the deep blue of seagoing uniform, but outstanding was the brilliant red of the robe worn by the Mayor, Councillor John Gwyther, who was supported by the Town Clerk and two mace bearers. The ponderous maces were wrapped in black crepe, which sybolised the sorrow the five tragic deaths has occasioned. While the assembly stood bareheaded, the first part of the funeral service was conducted by the Rev J.T. Morgan MA.

Later, headed by the deputy chief of police and a police sergeant, a procession was formed which wended its way slowly to the outskirts of the town. Firemen from other towns walked four abreast; auxiliary firemen in oilskins and knee boots helped to swell the gathering. Here and there a medal glittered; here and there massive brass helmets trapped the shafts of light which lit up the scene. The dominant note was one of solemnity and tranquil resignation. Four firemen walked on either side of the bier, all friends of the deceasd. Amongst those who paid their last token were the mayors of neighbouring towns, and a number of public officials, including Captain Thomas Breaks, Chief Inspector of Fire Brigades, and the fire chiefs of a number of brigades.

What the writer didn't add was at that very time the inferno was raging worse than ever, and that the morale of the firefighters was reaching near breaking point. As he walked with head bowed in that slow, sad procession through Pembroke Dock, Captain Thomas Breaks was wondering just how much more the men could take before they cracked completely.

CHAPTER SIX

AUGUST 23RD – 31ST

Pillar of fire

There was a line of firemen up by the moat, gyrating like chickens on a spit. They had to keep turning because they couldn't face that terrible heat for more than a couple of seconds at a time...

Fireman Len Haggar, Pembroke.

The deaths of the Cardiff men under such horrifying circumstances had a devastating effect on morale. Still hopelessly under-strength to cope with such a gigantic blaze, the firemen had also endured aerial attack and many felt they couldn't take any more.

When flaming oil from the burst tank rapidly spread, the men retreated in confusion and disorder, and although they eventually re-grouped to bring things under control, another major leak from the mortally wounded tank brought further crisis in the late afternoon and early evening.

Another view from Neyland of the huge pall of smoke which towered over South Pembrokeshire from the inferno. *(Roy Hordley)*

Rumour fast gained momentum that 60 firemen had died in the deteriorating conditions, and the story was treated so seriously that a fleet of ambulances, with Betty Davies at the wheel of one, police cars, military vehicles, off-duty fire personnel and anxious relatives and friends, all rushed to Pennar.

The sheer volume of their number caused chaos along the route, and a certain amount of panic within the depot itself, where isolated pockets of firemen, after learning about the rumour and spotting the size of the "rescue" party, feared it to be true.

But Captain Breaks, chiefs of various brigades, and Admiralty and dockyard officials, managed to restore order. The emergency services and others, when told the true circumstances and assured that no more lives had been lost, rapidly dispersed to advise the desperately worried inhabitants of Pembroke Dock of the reality of the situation.

Throughout the remainder of that week 450 firemen from different English brigades, including Birmingham, Bristol, Cheltenham and Gloucester, poured into Pembroke Dock until a total of 22 brigades and some 650 men were actively involved in the stupendous firefight. The size of the contingents ranged from over 100 in the case of Bristol, to four from Stroud in Gloucester – which happened to be the total strength of that town's fire service!

After the war it was learned that the Llanreath inferno produced the first ever large-scale movement of firemen and fire appliances in Britain. However, although reasonably well briefed in advance, nothing really prepared the newcomers for what awaited them at Pembroke Dock.

Mrs Eleanor Morse waved to the English firemen as they streamed past her home at 1 Military Road, Pennar, on fire engines and support appliances still gleaming from spit and polish, despite the many miles they'd covered to get to the south-west corner of Wales.

The men were jabbing their thumbs in the air, and some sang and joked as they vanished into the smoke at the top of the street to link up with their Welsh comrades. It was as if, another onlooker remarked at the time, they'd been instructed to put on a bright and breezy show in order to lift the decidedly sagging spirits of the people – at least those still left in Pennar.

Three days later Mrs Morse and her near neighbours watched small groups of them coming back down the road on foot. They were completely unrecognisable from the men they'd seen arrive in dashing helmets and spick and span uniforms. They were saturated with oil and their clothing was in tatters. Some were being half carried ; some swayed like drunken men; others with bandages swathing their oil-damaged eyes, were gently

Mrs Eleanor Morse, who watched the English brigades arrive in Pennar "looking spic and span".
(Mrs Nancy Thomas)

guided by comrades. All had the appearance of shell-shocked troops; of men who'd been to hell and back.

A number couldn't walk at all because oil had got into their boots, and transport, including motor cycles with sidecars, had been pressed into service to convey them to the casualty stations and rest centres. No one was surprised to see so many coming in for care and attention because by then, in spite of the reinforcements, a third of the Llanreath oil fuel depot was ablaze.

One hundred men of the Birmingham fire brigade slipped out of the city on the evening of Thursday the 22nd. It was the first regional call of the war for the Midlanders and they were in excellent spirits. They had no knowledge that the fire they were going to help to fight had claimed five lives earlier that day.

The reflection of the holocaust in the night sky attracted their attention while the convoy of appliances was still 100 miles from Pembroke Dock, and the sight shook them considerably.

After daybreak on Friday they were able to examine for themselves the whole area of devastation, and their reaction was no different to that of other newly arrived brigades; shock, and a gut feeling that maybe they were taking on more than they could chew.

The air was thick with smuts and foul with the reek of burning oil. By then the cavernous moat was partly filled with water on which floated a great mass of oil. Poultry, pigs, dogs, cats, birds, buildings and every bit of vegetation were all coated in black, oily scum. Three tanks blazed furiously while two others, which had collapsed, were being allowed to burn themselves out.

Tom Breaks had persisted with the tactic employed by Chief Arthur Morris at the outset – keeping the burning tanks in isolation – and one of

One of the most graphic pictures associated with the fire is this one of local firemen assembled in Treowen Road, Pennar, after coming off shift. They are about to answer a roll-call to ensure all are present, and safe and sound. The weariness of the men is all too evident, but they still stand smartly to attention. Some are wearing slippers, an indication that oil had seeped into their boots, and the firemen on the extreme right of the front rank appears to be bare-footed. Some of the men are bare-headed. There are at least four fire chiefs (wearing the white shoulder flash) in the line-up, and Chief Arthur Morris is the tall figure in the centre of the front rank. The equally tall fireman third to his right is believed to be Alan Murray, who arrived in Pembrokeshire a year before the war to player-manage Milford football club. He had previously played for Bolton Wanderers and Bristol Rovers. He served with the Milford brigade for the duration of the war and some years afterwards. In the background (right) is Pennar School where many firemen were billeted. Smoke from the fire blankets the skyline beyond.

(John Arter)

the first steps taken by the Birmingham firemen when they moved in, was to set up a number of monitor branches. These produced extra powerful streams, and were positioned around the blazing tanks to form a heavy ring of water through which flames could not pass.

But this system did not allow for what happened on the night of Saturday the 24th, when there was a spectacular "boil over". The effects, not unsimilar to a nuclear explosion of the modern age, were so devastating they brought people out of their homes all over West Wales as the whole sky turned a vivid orangy-red.

There was a warning rumble which developed into a mighty roar and then oil surged over the top of a burning tank, ran down the moat, across the water and – as incredible as it now seems – up the other side before advancing on the depot reservation itself. Almost instantly the whole mass became incandescent – an immense pillar of fire some 1,000 feet high and, on the ground, a river of blazing oil 100 feet wide and 1,000 feet long.

Firemen dropped everything and ran for their lives towards the high ground. Many made it in the nick of time, suffering nothing more serious than scorching. Considering there must have been as many as 400 fire personnel in the depot that night, it was an act of providence no one was cremated alive, and that there wasn't even a casualty with burns worth talking about.

Fireman Sid Hay, Pembroke, was with a number of others down on Llanreath beach pumping sea water, and recalled "The word went out that burning oil was flowing like a river down the valley towards the beach. We got out of there so fast the suctions were dragging behind the pumps all the way up Llanreath hill. In the panic nobody had bothered to release them".

Harry Jones, a Milford fireman, was also at Llanreath and remembered "There was supposed to be burning oil pouring down the valley. It certainly looked that way and a lot of us were fooled. We really believed we were goners. In fact, it was an illusion created by the smoke and flame following the 'boil over' ".

Pembroke Dock fire chief Arthur Morris had been right about the moat. It had granted men precious seconds to take to their heels. Without the moat scores of firefighters, perhaps hundreds, would have burned to death that night. As it was thousands of pounds worth of hose lines, pumps and other valuable equipment, were lost in that wild, nightmarish retreat to safety.

By dawn on Sunday strenuous and often valiant efforts on the part of dog-tired firemen (off-duty personnel had been rushed to the scene as well) brought what had been a desperately alarming situation under a considerable measure of control.

What no one was prepared for, following that night of terror, was another visit by the Luftwaffe. Round about 1.30pm on Sunday the 25th, a single aircraft – identified as a Ju 88 – attempted to dive-bomb the tanks but failed to cause any damage, although three firemen were injured. All the bombs fell wide of the depot, but were sufficiently near to send firefighters scurrying for shelter, especially as the German bomber also peppered the site with machine-gun fire.

Tommy Gibby was lying low next to another Pembroke Dock fireman, Tommy Warburton, and recalled "Bullets were zipping all around and one took Tommy's knuckle off. He got up bleeding like a stuck pig, and shaking his wounded fist at the sky, screamed 'That's close enough you

This photograph, taken during the height of the fire, shows three members of the Tenby brigade, W. P. "Bill" English, Stanley Thomas and Bill Anderson, in Pembroke Street, Pembroke Dock. At the top of the street smoke drifts across the Barracks Hill. The tall building on the left is now the Dolphin Hotel. Bill English is the well remembered Tenby photographer. Bill Anderson was a plumber and Stanley Thomas an undertaker! They were obviously off-duty at the time, but hardly in their Sunday best! (Mrs Doris English)

bastards – that's close enough! 'He then broke down and cried. The men were under enormous stress and strain".

George Fish and Glanville Evans of Pembroke Dock, saw the plane and when someone yelled "Look out, it's a Jerry!" ducked under a wooden billet-like structure used as a store. Fish remembered "As we lay there after the bombing, not knowing whether the plane was still around or not, we heard a rustlling, squeaking noise and were shocked to see an army of rats coming towards us. They'd been frightened by the bombs. We kept absolutely still – to be honest we were petrified – and they passed us by and ran into the open. We both agreed afterwards we'd rather face Jerry any day!"

The first bomb dropped by the attacking aircraft uprooted a telegraph pole just outside the depot which, by a freak, landed point downwards a few yards away to resume its previous upright position!

This extraordinary sight was witnessed by Milford Haven fireman Jack Philpin, who recalled "I thought I was seeing things! I remember thinking 'I know I'm whacked out and dead tired, but this is bloody ridiculous!' "

There was a fair amount of enemy air activity around the West Wales coast that Sunday.

In the early evening Jack Thomas, duty officer at St Govan's coastguard station, about 10 miles from Pembroke Dock, trained his binoculars on aircraft attacking shipping on the horizon. He saw one plane, unable to pull out of a dive, plummet into the sea with a tremendous splash.

Then Thomas focused on a Spitfire which, as it drew nearer, appeared to be in trouble. The fighter, swinging from side to side and trailing a thin line of smoke, just managed to clear the cliffs west of the medieval St Govan's Chapel, before crash-landing close to Crickmail Farm.

Bert Brace was in the farmhouse when he heard aircraft engines. Outside he saw two Spitfires circling very low nearby. He headed in that direction, came across the crashed aircraft, and then saw the pilot tottering towards him. When the farmer asked if he was alright, he mumbled "That's the third bugger I've pranged this week!"

The badly shocked flier was Flight Lieutenant Bob Stanford Tuck of 92 Squadron, based at RAF Pembrey in Carmarthenshire, one of the RAF's top aces in the Battle of Britain, and a man said to have Lady Luck as his co-pilot! He had, indeed, been involved in two other crashes earlier in the week, and on both occasions had destroyed an enemy aircraft before coming to grief himself.

While on patrol early on Sunday evening the 25th, Tuck saw the smoke from the oil tanks fire and noted "Between 3,000 and 4,000 feet there was a solid shelf of white cloud, and running through it was a distinct oily black ribbon".

Not long afterwards he was ordered to intercept a Dornier Do 17 bomber – known to the RAF as the "Flying Pencil" – reported to be attacking a British merchant vessel near St Govan's lightship. The German struck first, damaging the Spitfire's engine with a hail of bullets, but Tuck managed a quick burst of fire from only 25 yards and the Dornier later crashed off Land's End. Two other 92 Squadron pilots, Bobby Holland

John James (right) and Fred Dyson with the aircraft part found after the Spitfire crash. It was found by Fred Dyson's father, Arthur, not far from the scene of the crash. (Fred Dyson)

and Roy Mottram, saw Tuck "safely" down and then circled the crashed Spitfire to ensure he was still in one piece, and to alert local people.

The roar of their engines led to the Vicar, the Rev Rees, and his flock at Bosherston Church, hurrying outside to see what the commotion was all about. It had been decided to abandon the service anyway, because the noise had drowned the vicar's sermon!

The RAF, like the Luftwaffe, was no respecter of the Sabbath!

Two members of the Bosherston congregation, Fred Dyson and Lewis John, saw the Spitfires were repeatedly circling over Crickmail and set off in that direction. They found the wrecked fighter lying at an angle on a hedgebank, the vaporising fuel making it appear to be steaming. The cockpit canopy was open, but there was no sign of the pilot. The two men, assuming he had baled out, wondered whether he was dead or alive?

By then Tuck, only semi-conscious, was being conveyed to the Royal Navy hospital at Fort Road, Pembroke Dock, where he was detained overnight suffering from shock and knee injuries. Less than a quarter of a mile away hundreds of firemen were engaged in their massive task.

Some days later Fred Dyson's father, Arthur, discovered part of the cockpit canopy believed to be from Tuck's wrecked Spitfire. For the next 25 years it was used as a potato shed window at a nearby farm, before being passed on to local farmer John James, in whose possession it has remained to this day.

Bob Stanford Tuck went on to attain the rank of Wing Commander, and was credited with 29 enemy aircraft destroyed. He was awarded the DSO, DFC, and two bars. This officer was one of the most skilful – and certainly one of the luckiest – Battle of Britain pilots, who became an RAF legend in the early part of the war. His luck ran out in January 1942 when he crash-landed near German anti-aircraft batteries on the outskirts of Boulogne, and was taken prisoner. He spent the remainder of the war in a PoW camp.

Battle of Britain ace Bob Stanford Tuck, who survived when his Spitfire crashed close to Crickmail Farm.

On Monday evening, August 26th, Pembroke Borough councillors attended a special meeting called to consider the payment of extra money to the Pembroke Dock and Pembroke brigades.

The *Guardian* subsequently reported "Appreciation of the heroic and gallant work performed by the firemen was repeatedly expressed. The meeting was presided over by Alderman John Hay, and the Fire Chief, Mr Arthur Morris, said between 40 and 50 local men were lending assistance.

Councillor W. J. Phillips felt they all deserved decorations equal to those earned on the battlefield, because the men had been carrying their lives in their hands. Several other councillors added their tribute, and it was decided that all local AFS and regular firemen should be paid at the rate of three pounds, fifty shillings per week, and that application be made to the Home Office to pay a higher scale. It was further resolved that the brigade be increased to 34 regular men.

Present at that meeting was Bill Richards, Haverfordwest, then a young Pembroke Dock-based reporter for the *Guardian*.

He later wrote "Those who attended will never forget the appearance of Mr Arthur Morris, who took an hour off from his grim task to report to the council. Beneath the grime which he had not had time to wash off, his pale, drawn face told eloquently of the ordeal the men were suffering. He was unshaven and his eyes were heavy and red-rimmed. As the meeting progressed it was noticed that on several occasions he almost fell asleep".

Throughout the second week the Herculean efforts to keep the fire in check went on around the clock. But continuing eruptions – firemen likened them to milk in a saucepan boiling over – made it very much a losing battle.

Taken on August 31st –
12 days after the raid –
and shot from a
considerable height, this
photograph shows all but
six of the tanks burning.
The diamond-shaped
building to the right of
the column of smoke is
the Defensible Barracks.
A number of flying-boats
are moored off the RAF
station, and another off
Pembroke Ferry, at the
top of the picture.
(The National Assembly
for Wales)

Another aerial
photograph, this time
from a low level, shows
firemen directing jets at
a burning tank, top
left. There are four
bomb craters in the
field just outside the
depot.
(The National
Assembly for Wales)

Tank after tank ignited until eight were blazing simultaneously, while three others were burning themselves out. It was at this time that "Devil's Kitchen" became a commonly used expression to sum up the harrowing conditions at the depot. And residents of Pembroke Dock lived in daily fear of an exceptional eruption cascading flaming oil on to the town.

As it was, only a wall of sandbags saved a number of men from one of the most horrifying deaths imaginable in the underground tunnel which linked the depot with the dockyard below.

A sea of burning oil crept towards the tunnel, but the sandbags which had been piled there for that very purpose held firm. If they had been swept aside, the men would have had to stampede down the tunnel in a macabre race for safety, praying they would reach the other end before that awful, slithering, flaming mass embraced them.

Casualties, some serious, increased considerably. A number of firemen, including one injured in an attack by enemy aircraft, were admitted to hospital but the great majority were attended to by St John Ambulance and Red Cross workers, who were themselves dead tired and at breaking point.

Acts of heroism in that hellish cauldron were common enough, but an outstanding feat of bravery was performed by Leading Fireman George Knight of the Birmingham Auxiliary Fire Service on Sunday August 25th.

A tank was burning inside and scalding oil gushed from a hole near the top. It seemed almost certain that unless this was plugged the tank would catch fire altogether and produce another highly dangerous "boil-over". After several unsuccessful plugging attempts, Knight volunteered, saying "I'll have a shot at it".

A 30 foot ladder was run up against the side of the tank and above the depression, which was filled with warm oil. Then the Birmingham man, carrying a wooden plug, climbed to the top in near impossible conditions because he was being sprayed all the time with hot oil. With some difficulty he managed to wedge the plug in and stem the flow, his achievement considerably lessening the danger of the oil in the "saucer" igniting and spreading, and enabling his colleagues to concentrate more effectively on the tank. At any time he could have slipped and fallen from the ladder into the oil-filled depression below.

For his courage George Knight was awarded the George Medal.

By the third week a total of eleven tanks had gone up in flames. Some were completely destroyed, others still burning. But the firemen had succeeded in saving the remaining six and indeed, the situation had improved to such an extent that the large Birmingham contingent was withdrawn.

The end was in sight.

CHAPTER SEVEN

AFTERMATH

The cold shoulder

Those who subsequently received awards for the parts they played in the Llanreath depot inferno were all recommended by Captain Thomas Breaks, and because of this he became a controversial and, in some quarters, a much distrusted figure...

To the end the great fire spat defiance. On September 6th, just when it seemed it was all over, there were fears of another holocaust as a tank collapsed creating an enormous flare-up.

It also caused an adjoining tank, which had been smouldering for several days, to explode back into life with such a tremendous bang that windows rattled all over Pembrokeshire. But again the battle-hardened firemen regained control and a couple of nights later the curtain came down on the longest continuous major fire of the Second World War in Britain. There was a final, brief flurry of flame round about midnight

The success of the raid was a great propaganda coup for the Germans, and this picture of the blazing tanks appeared in 'Der Adler', the official magazine of the Luftwaffe. *(Lawswood Collection)*

which lit up the whole sky, and then darkness – natural darkness.

"If we hadn't felt so weary, we'd have cheered", said Fireman Frank John of Milford Haven. "But we were too tired; we were too damned tired".

In the final analysis, although some 650 firefighters had been through absolute hell and the civilian population had lived on a knife edge for three weeks, Pembroke Dock had been granted more luck than it could have dared hope for.

The duration of the oil tanks fire coincided with the climax of the Battle of Britain, to which the Germans committed most of their air force. If the traumatic struggle for supremacy in the vapour-trailed sky high above south-east England had not been waged at that particular time, there is no knowing how severe the follow-up bombing to the August 19th raid would have been.

After that attack the Germans returned on four occasions, once at night, with the intention of further bombing the tanks and harassing the emergency services. Each raid was carried out by a single aircraft, easily guided to the target by the 1,000 feet high tower of smoke. But thankfully, the accuracy of the bomb-aimers was poor, and while initially the machine-gunning caused some panic and concern, the planes never stayed around long enough to make the harassment really effective.

But a number of firemen from Bristol did have an incredibly lucky escape in the early hours of Monday September 6th when the spacious Temperance Hall, where they were billeted, was so badly damaged it was later demolished.

This attack had no connection with those directed against the tanks although the pilot of the aircraft, believed to have been a Dornier Do 17, used the brilliant light cast by the blaze at night to bomb Pembroke Dock with high explosives and incendiaries.

Extensive damage was caused to the Gwyther Street and Arthur Street areas, and in Lewis Street, where the Temperance Hall was sited, but there was not one fatality. A large number of off-duty firemen were sleeping in the hall and 18 were injured, two seriously. Only the four main walls were left standing, and it was an absolute miracle no one was killed.

Such bombing was always described as "indiscriminate", but it should be borne in mind that two barracks, Llanion and Defensible, the RAF flying boat station and naval dockyard, together with the other Admiralty oil tank depot at Llanion, on the opposite side of Pembroke Dock to Llanreath, were military targets all located within or on the perimeter of what was a small town. The risk to civilian life and property, therefore, was really unavoidable.

Other venues used to billet firemen included Pennar School, and Stan Israel, of Cardiff, remembered "Members of our brigade stayed there, and you couldn't see the floor at any time for sleeping men. There was absolutely no space left on the floor, and I had to curl up on a large mantlepiece. Others also had to improvise in order to find somewhere to lie down".

(When Pennar School eventually returned to normal the head teacher, with considerable under-statement, noted in the logbook on October 14th... "During the school holidays the oil tanks at Llanreath were bombed, and the school was used by parties of firemen fighting the fire".)

The casualties of the Temperance Hall bombing were visited in hospital by Captain Thomas Breaks who, before the end of that week, was the central figure in an embarrassing episode which was hushed up at the time and indeed, didn't receive public mention until 40 years later.

Satisfied his men had everything under control, Breaks decided to spend a few hours relaxing in the surrounding countryside, and borrowed a car for the purpose. He also changed into civilian clothing. Mentally and physically he was exhausted, which was almost certainly why the excursion landed him in trouble. For some reason he wandered off the beaten track near Merrion village and ended up on the army's tank-training range at Castlemartin, very close to where Bob Stanford Tuck crash-landed his Spitfire the previous month.

The sudden appearance of an unauthorised car immediately alerted the military and Corporal Douglas Gorton, 15th/19th Hussars, who had fought in the BEF's retreat to Dunkirk, was detailed to take an armed squad to apprehend the vehicle and its driver.

He later settled in Pembroke, and recalled "There were supposed to be spies about then, not to mention one or two local people allegedly sympathetic to the Nazi cause, and the army at Castlemartin was very edgy. Even a prominent figure in the agricultural community was being kept under observation because he was suspected of passing information on to the Germans.

"When we stopped the car we didn't recognise the driver, and he had no identity papers. He kept saying he was from the Home Office, and one of the lads chided 'Come on mate, you can think of a better one than that!' He was arrested, conveyed to the guardroom, and vigorously interrogated by Colonel Skinner, the commanding officer at Castlemartin. Some considerable time passed and quite a few telephone calls were made, before the man was able to positively identify himself as Captain Thomas Breaks from the Home Office".

Those who subsequently received awards for the parts they played in the Llanreath depot inferno were all recommended by Breaks, and because of this he became a controversial and, in some quarters, much distrusted figure.

Arthur Morris – overlooked when the awards list was drawn up.

Horace Howarth – awarded the B. E. M.

Milford Haven fire chief Matt Acornley received the George Medal, and the town clerk of Milford Urban District Council, Mr Horace Howarth, who was also commandant of the town brigade, got the British Empire Medal.

But for Chief Arthur Morris of Pembroke Dock, the man who assumed immediate command following the raid, and whose initial measures were largely responsible for preventing the fire incinerating Military Road, Owen Street and other parts of Pennar, there was no decoration. Morris, who did not go to bed for 17 days during the time the tanks blazed, had to make do with his name appearing on a list of commendations for "gallantry or good service in connection with civil defence".

To add insult to injury, Breaks wrote a letter to Chief Matt Acornley, a copy of which appeared in the local press. It read "I take this opportunity of placing on record my deep appreciation of the manner in which you, as District Officer, assumed control of a most serious and hazardous fire prior to the arrival of the Home Office Fire Brigade Division. I also thank you, and members of the brigade under your command, for the excellent service you rendered during the whole of the progress of the fire."

The truth of the matter was that because of his late arrival on the day of the raid, Acornley was very much in the hands of Morris, who was well familiar with the depot's layout, and whose early tactics prevented the one burning tank from igniting others. As regional fire officer, Acornley did out-rank Morris but all local firemen who were there during the first two days were adamant that the Pembroke Dock chief appeared to be directing things right up to the time of Breaks arrival.

Predictably, when they learned about the Milford awards – the only ones to come to Pembrokeshire – the reaction of Morris' men, and the people of Pembroke Dock and Pembroke, was one of outrage. Their anger, resentment and jealousy was understandable.

Britain's biggest inferno since the Great Fire of London in 1666 had burned for three weeks at Pembroke Dock. The public needed heroes very badly in 1940, and the people of Pembroke Dock and Pembroke were firmly of the opinion they had a very special one in Arthur Morris. He was regarded as a traditional hero, quiet and unassuming in the "Cometh the hour, cometh the man" mould.

And he had been cold-shouldered by the establishment.

"Pomp" Morris, as he was affectionately known to his men, must have been deeply hurt by the snub, but for the rest of his days – he died in 1970 – steadfastly refused to be drawn into discussion about the oil tanks fire awards. If the former fire chief, tall, sturdily built, and with a weather – beaten face, knew the reason why he was overlooked for a medal, and many suspected he did, he carried it with him to the grave.

One of Morris' firemen, Tom Gibby, who became a senior staff officer with the West Riding of Yorkshire Fire Service after the war, had this to say about his old boss in the summer of 1980 – the 40th anniversary of the raid:

"It is distressing for me, and indeed, all others who served with him, to recall that Chief Morris was literally cast aside when the gallantry awards were allocated. The Tom Breaks reasoning was difficult to accept, but with hindsight was completely in keeping with that most controversial officer who was not even at the fire during its initial stages. What we do know is that Arthur Morris was not a yes-man, and that he called a spade a spade. The answer as to why he was overlooked when the awards list was drawn up could be hidden in those special qualities.

"Not once in my 30 years with the fire

Matt Acornley – received the George Medal.

Captain Thomas Breaks, Chief Inspector of the Fire Brigades Division at the Home Office, and the man in charge of the oil tanks fire-fight. He was to become a controversial figure with local firemen.

(Mike George)

service did I meet an officer with so much courage and integrity, and who was so devoted to his duty. His leadership, particularly in times of stress, was of the highest order. Indeed, I shall always consider it a privilege to have served under him. I shall always remember him for his coolness in dangerous situations, and for his gallantry, not only at the oil tanks fire but also during the heavy air raids on Pembroke Dock during the winter of 1940-41, and the summer of '41. I am sure everyone else who served with Arthur Morris share these sentiments. We knew and admired him for what he was; a very brave officer devoted to his duty, and it is scandalous those special qualities were never officially recognised".

Scandal of a totally different kind was also attached to the awards controversy. It centred around a fire officer from an English brigade whose bravery and general conduct through-out the tanks blaze had resulted in him being recommended for the George Medal, and promotion. But this was immediately cancelled when he was found, by a senior officer, in bed with a female member of the fire service on brigade premises.

Matt Acornley was the first fire chief to come to Pembrokeshire on a full – time basis, and his

The 'Western Telegraph's' account of the raid. The heading "Dock attacked by bombers" was as close as the paper could get to saying oil tanks at Pembroke Dock were the target.

DOCK ATTACKED BY BOMBERS

OIL TANK SET ON FIRE

THREE JUNKERS IN RAID

'A dock in South Wales was attacked by enemy bombers on Monday after-noon, and an Air Ministry and Ministry of Home Security communique stated :
" But the damage was confined to an oil tank, which was set on fire. There were no casualties.";

Three Junkers 88 are believed to have taken part in the raid.

Spitfires went up in pursuit and anti-aircraft batteries went into action.

An unconfirmed report stated that one 'plane was brought down at sea. No confirmation was possible in the area, though one of the enemy machines was seen by townspeople beating a hasty retreat with smoke pouring from its tail.

The aeroplane dived from the sun and dropped eight bombs. A labourer, who was 100 yards from where the bombs fell, was blown over a fence but was unhurt. Six workmen at the tanks, two watchmen and a cashier who was hand-ing out vouchers, escaped injury ; in fact not one casualty was reported.

The bombs dropped not far from a crowded residential area, but there was a total absence of panic ; in fact the coolness with which the people in the neghbourhood faced the danger was truly amazing.

Within a few minutes they were on the doorsteps discussing the attack, and in a very short time people from out-side the district began to visit the scenes of the air raid.

COURAGE OF LITTLE CHILDREN.

The spirit of the people is best typified by the little children who were picking blackberries just over the road when the raiders dropped their salvo. Displaying great courage, the small men and women of tomorrow sought shelter, where they contentedly re-mained until the raid was over. Their

rough time. All he wanted was to get away, and get away he did, with the two Spitfires after him. The three of them vanished in the distance but I am confident that our machines brought that bomber down before he got very far."

FIREMEN MACHINE-GUNNED.

Several firemen are reported to have been injured by machine gun fire. One fireman from Swansea was struck in the ribs by a machine gun bullet, and a number of people are suffering from shock. A Captain of one of the brigades told a "Telegraph" reporter :
" I was engaged as a fireman at a munition works during the last war. Believe me, I saw something then, but it is nothing to compare with what I and others went through this morning.
" We were all fighting the flames for dear life," he went on, "when a Jerry bomber dived from behind the dense clouds of smoke, scored another direct hit and then swooped down to 100 yards and machine gunned us. We all fell flat on the ground and some scrambled under-neath the pumps and fire engines. It was terrible, and I think there were four men taken to hospital."

A number of people moved to a near-by seaside resort, where they slept in their cars. Before leaving their homes they took with them blankets and other personal belongings.

One Army officer who saw distin-guished service during the Great War, was out throughout Monday night with a rifle. "I was determined to have a pot at a German plane if it came with-in range.

A.R.P. services were busy from dawn until dark on Tuesday and many of them remained on duty during the night.

76

training methods earned him the respect of Milford firemen. Frank John remembered him as "A chief who nurtured some good practical firemen, and who established a good reputation for the Milford brigade".

No one in Pembroke Dock really begrudged him the George Medal. It was the fact their own chief, who was at the scene of the fire well before his Milford counterpart, was not similarly honoured, which so infuriated the public.

Mr Acornley left Milford in the immediate post-war years and following his death in the 1970s, the George Medal and some of his wartime possessions were offered for sale in Glasgow. This news filtered back to Pembrokeshire and a move was made to enter a bid for the medal on behalf of the Dyfed Fire Brigade, but it fell though.

The Milford brigade commandant, Horace Howarth, was a popular figure with the town's wartime firemen, and a highly efficient and most affable town clerk. But his award of the British Empire Medal produced a barrage of criticism on the grounds that compared with other senior fire personnel, he spent very little time at the tanks inferno.

In addition to Chief Acornley, others who received the George Medal were Fire Sergeant Daniel James Collins, Cardiff Fire Brigade; Sub Officer William Brown and Leading Fireman Norman Groom, Cardiff Auxiliary Fire Service; and Leading Fireman George Knight, Birmingham Auxiliary Fire Service, along with eight Bristol firemen. Awards of the MBE were made to Mr M. C. Sadler, Patrol Officer, Bristol Auxiliary Fire Service; and Mr A. R. B. Hart, Newport Fire Brigade. Breaks himself was awarded the OBE on the recommendation of the Home Secretary.

The tanks blaze should have provided local newspaper reporters with the most sensational story of their working lives. But on Wednesday August 21st, the morning Tom Breaks arrived in Pembroke Dock, all the *Telegraph* could muster was a heavily censored account of the raid two days previously. The *Guardian* carried a similar report on Friday the 23rd.

Both papers stated that three Ju 88s had attacked a south-west Wales town causing damage to an oil tank, and the *Telegraph* added "Although bombs were dropped close to a crowded residential area, there was a total absence of panic" – which was far removed from the truth.

Another part of the *Telegraph* report read "An army officer who saw distinguished service in the 1914-18 War, was out and about throughout Monday night with a rifle, determined to have a pot at any German aircraft which might return to the scene."

Every *Telegraph* and *Guardian* reader knew the oil tank fire was at Pembroke Dock, but because of the strict censorship law the papers were forbidden to say so. Instead they and the two other Pembrokeshire newspapers, the *Tenby Observer* and *Fishguard Echo*, had to resort to patriotic drivel which, while appearing nonsensical now, suited the mood of the time when everyone was encouraged to keep a stiff upper lip.

Members of the Pembroke Dock St John Ambulance Division with their Superintendent, Mrs I. P. Hammond (seated centre), who were on duty throughout the fire. In the group are Miss Jones (then a member of the staff of the old Pembroke Dock County School), Doreen Powiss, Gwen Sullivan, Sally Peel-Hobson, Madge Thompson, Maud Medwell, Jennie Noakes, Lily Thomas, Nurse Knight, Mrs Blackmore, Mrs Dew, Linda Head and Molly Browning. Mrs Hammond was eventually awarded the BEM for her work on behalf of the Pembroke Dock division. *(Author's Collection)*

There were many heroines during those dark days, none more than the womenfolk of Pennar. After St Patrick's Church Sunday School had been opened as a first-aid post and casualty station for the firemen, housewives – many with husbands in the armed forces – cared for them as best they could, heating water in gas boilers and shuttling it across to the church hall for the exhausted men to wash and scrub off the grime.

Pennar had no hot water on tap then, nor baths as we know them today. Families had to make do with gas boilers and "tin" baths. Until the Pembroke Dock Food Office, in charge of Mr Frank Sudbury, became operational, the Pennar ladies shared their family food rations with the firemen – a tremendous sacrifice, and one which the recipients, from different parts of Britain, never forgot.

Other angels of mercy were the St John Ambulance Division under Mrs Phyllis Hammond, Nurse Knight and Doctor Evan Jones, and Mrs Greathead's Pembroke Red Cross detachment. This detachment did day duty at its Pennar post throughout the fire, while the St John Division was on duty day and night in Pennar.

A member of the St John team, Miss Sally Peel-Hobson (later Mrs Neil), recalled "During the long hours firemen would come in dog-tired, grimy and dripping with perspiration. I remember their anxiety on the day the Cardiff firemen were killed. Our worse night was when the message came through that the Temperance Hall had been bombed. Not long afterwards at least 30 very traumatised firemen arrived from the hall, or what was left of it. They had cuts and bruises, and their uniforms were plastered with dust and embedded with tiny splinters of glass. Even in their shocked state they were all aware they'd had a very close brush with death".

All of the men on duty at the tanks fire never forgot the hospitality and attention they received. A member of the Birmingham contingent later wrote "We have very happy memories of the way people took us to their hearts, of the untiring efforts of the local women at the church hall, who bathed our eyes, gave us clean socks after cutting the oil – saturated ones off, and providing simple comforts, and sometimes a little piano music to accompany our snatched midnight meal. We remember, too, how for the first time since we donned our uniforms in 1939, we were treated by the naval and military authorities with some degree of respect and understanding".

After their return home the officer – in – charge of the Bristol party, sent the following message to the people of Pembroke Dock:

"Words are totally inadequate to express the gratitude which the men of Bristol feel towards you. The reception we had, and the attention showered upon us by you wonderful people, has really been stupendous. When we left Bristol we knew we were heading for a difficult and extremely dangerous task. We expected that we would have to endure all kinds of hardship, that we would have to sleep out "on the job" in all sorts of conditions, and that we would have to exist on the iron rations we had with us. Instead, we were given the most overwhelming hospitality. Everything was done for us. We were given every comfort, and the good ladies even went so far as to bathe our feet. In all our experience we have never known such kindness, and we do ask you to accept thanks which comes from the very bottom of our hearts".

Hundreds of birds, and wild and domestic animals perished as the result of the great fire, a fact largely overlooked at that time because of its magnitude, and the effect it had on humans.

But in his monthly column for September 1940, the *Guardian's* nature notes contributor, H. R. Chubb, did have this to say :

"I have often wondered in these days and nights of air raids, what effect bombs have on bird and beast? What does the rabbit feel and do when the earth about him rocks violently, and the sides of his deep burrow cave in when a bomb tears a great hole in the ground not far away?

"Domestic creatures, as well as wild animals and birds, are terrified of thunder and lightning, more so than humans, perhaps because their senses are more keenly attuned to climatic and atmospheric conditions. How much more devastating to their alert senses, their sensitive ears, and to their comparitively frail organisms then, must be the sudden, shattering, earth rocking roar of high explosives in the middle of the night?

"Rabbits, moles, stoats, badgers and otters must die in their subterranean retreats when the reeling ground hurls them against the sides of their lairs, and one can easily imagine the effect of blast and concussion on peacefully sleeping birds in the branches of trees".

These smartly uniformed Milford Haven firemen were pictured in July 1940 with the then chairman of the town's urban district council, Councillor Ivor Phillips, seated centre. Mr Phillips, for many years headmaster of Milford Central School, is flanked by the brigade's commandant, Mr Horace Howarth, and fire chief Matt Acornley. The identity of the "mascot", seen in front of the council chairman, is not known. At the time this photograph was taken the Milford Brigade was advertising for new recruits. (Raymond Evans)

CHAPTER EIGHT

WHERE WAS THE RAF ?

We had no guns, the RAF weren't around when we needed them and, to cap everything, by the time the siren sounded Jerry had been and gone.
Section Leader Harry Baker, Pembroke Dock Fire Brigade.

In its censored account of the raid the *Telegraph* stated that anti – aircraft guns went into action, and that the enemy aircraft were pursued by Spitfires. It added that one of the German planes was seen "beating a hasty retreat with smoke pouring from its tail", and that an unconfirmed report indicated that the same aircraft was brought down over the sea.

This was pure propaganda. There were no guns defending Pembroke Dock. Indeed, in August 1940 there were only three anti-aircraft batteries in the whole of South Wales and these were located at Llandarcy, Newport, and Barry.

A month prior to the attack the county's MP, Major Gwilym Lloyd George, visited Pembroke in response to heated complaints from the borough council that although Pembroke Dock, home to all three branches of the armed forces, was very much in harm's way, the area was completely undefended.

The news from the MP was disturbing, and shocked many councillors. He revealed that because of the huge losses sustained by the BEF during its retreat to Dunkirk, Britain was practically defenceless. Pembroke Dock would have to wait its turn for anti – aircraft guns and, he warned, they might be a long time coming.

Reporter Bill Richards, present at the meeting for the *Guardian*, recalled that for national security reasons even a hint of this shattering news was out of the question, and so no mention of it appeared in the press.

Lack of fighter cover during the fire, plus the fact the Ju 88s flew to Pembroke Dock unchallenged by Spitfire or Hurricane, came in for fierce criticism and many of the firemen, who'd been bombed and machine-gunned, echoed the words of British troops at Dunkirk "Where was the RAF?"

Stationed at Pembrey with 92 Spitfire Squadron was Pilot Officer (later Squadron Leader) Anthony Bartley, who in a letter to his father dated June 25th 1940, wrote "I am afraid the fighter boys are in very bad odour at the moment over the Dunkirk evacuation operations. The BEF have started stories that they never saw a single fighter the whole time they were being bombed. Some fighter pilots got roughed up by the army in pub brawls".

The Pembroke Dock public was also highly critical that RAF Fighter

Command appeared to be ignoring their plight. But in fairness to 92 Squadron, they had to protect a sector encompassing Bristol, Cardiff and Swansea, particularly at night, so that their hands were full.

It should be pointed out as well that 24 hours prior to the oil tanks raid, 92's "A" Flight was sent temporarily to Bibury in Gloucestershire, it being felt that this airfield was better placed than the squadron's West Wales base for the night defence of the Midlands. Thus Pembrey was left thin on the ground for Spitfires.

The next day, by an incredible coinsidence, Bibury was bombed at the same time as the oil tanks attack, by a Ju 88 from the same staffeln (squadron) as the three Pembroke Dock raiders.

Pilot Officer Bartley, one of the pilots who moved to Bibury, remembered "The attack came without warning (shades of Pembroke Dock!). I had just finished a luncheon sandwich, and was watching what I thought was an Oxford trainer circle the airfield when, to my horror, it dived down on our dispersal point, bombing and machine-gunning. Everything was obliterated by smoke and debris afterwards, and the Ju 88 rear–gunner fired a parting burst as his aircraft disappeared into cloud".

Bartley's Spitfire and another were damaged, and two others had to be written off. Immediately afterwards, two 92 pilots gave chase and shot down the Junkers some distance away – over the Solent. In this encounter the engine of a Spitfire piloted by Flight Lieutenant T. S. Wade, was hit by return fire and as Wade was preparing to force – land in a field, the engine ignited and fumes seeped into the cockpit. He brought the aircraft down in a wheels-up landing, leapt out, and raced away just seconds before it exploded into pieces.

The author has included these facts because although Pembrey was only a short distance from Pembroke Dock in terms of flying time, its pilots were always fully stretched, and 92 Squadron was also losing its share of aircraft through enemy action. Witness the three destroyed on August 18th. The squadron could not be everywhere at once.

On Sunday August 25th for example, when a German plane attempted to bomb the Llanreath tanks in the early afternoon, there wasn't an RAF fighter in sight. Yet some four hours later three Spitfires, including the one flown by Bob Stanford Tuck, engaged enemy aircraft off the South Pembrokeshire coast and destroyed at least one, losing Tuck's Spitfire in the process. As Tuck was to point out, it was a question of being in the right place at the right time, and quite often flying schedules didn't work that way.

Two Spitfires were scrambled at Pembrey when news was received that the tanks had been bombed, but the Germans got away unscathed and because of the success of the operation were subsequently feted at their French base, and later in Germany. Aerial photographs of the fire appeared in *Signal* and other Nazi propaganda publications, and the

A post-war view of the tanks site taken on April 15th 1946. The six tanks which survived the fire are on the right. Three more appeared to have been partially repaired. This photograph shows how close the hamlet of Llanreath, directly below the tank depot, was to the blaze. (The National Assembly for Wales)

Luftwaffe magazine *Der Adler*. The three crews were decorated by Reich-Marshall Hermann Goring, ranked second only to Hitler in the Nazi hierarchy, and head of the Luftwaffe. They had done their duty well – bombing one tank and, in the final analysis, destroying 11, as photographs taken by German reconnaissance aircraft were to show.

The delay in not sounding the siren until after the bombing caused a huge outcry and led to a number of people threatening to take the law into their own hands when German aircraft next appeared. Two persons mentioned in this narrative, Councillor J. R. Williams and Section Leader Harry Baker of the Pembroke Dock Fire Brigade, were later severely censured for setting off the siren without permission, but in mitigation it could be argued that their action may have saved lives.

Ted Owens… "pinched apples for the firemen".
(Mrs Mary Owens)

Baker was particularly incensed about the siren situation, and took his concern to Captain Tom Breaks. Complaining about the raid on the tanks, he asserted "We had no guns, the RAF weren't around when we needed them, and to cap everything the siren didn't sound until after Jerry had been and gone!"

The Home Office official could only sympathise, although privately he was deeply angry there was no protection for his men against attacks from the air, and vented that anger in official circles. Indeed, following his return to London, Breaks emphasised the pressing need for defences at places like Pembroke Dock with its many military targets, including a huge flying boat station, and this may well have influenced the decision to send anti–aircraft guns to the area much sooner than anticipated.

Almost certainly the youngest person on duty on the first three days of the fire was Ted Owens of Pembroke Dock. He was a few weeks short of his 16th birthday and had left school at the end of the spring term 1940. Ted was a messenger boy for the AFS but admitted in later years "I also raided the orchards of Llanreath village on behalf of the firemen, dodging the soldiers acting as guards. The firemen were very hungry and would eat anything edible. I collected the apples in a pillow-case.

"It was pinching of course, but for a very good cause! Because of the wind's direction not a lot of oil fell on Llanreath, but I still had to clean the apples with items left on various clothes lines – and they weren't exactly spotless either – before handing them over to the firemen. I also obtained a lot of bottles from the various empty houses, filled them with tap water and again, in a pillow-case, took them up to the firemen. They were parched all the time and could not drink enough water".

In 1943 Ted Owens joined the Royal Marines and on D-Day, after storming ashore with 41 Commando, was wounded on Sword Beach, removed to a hospital ship, and taken back with many other British casualties to England. He made a full recovery and just over two months later rejoined his unit on the France-Belgium border.

⸻⸻

The great fire produced some interesting statistics. Twenty-two brigades, comprising approximately 650 men, used 53 pumps and nine miles of hose. The men were fed at a cost of £850, and the telephone bill at Pembroke Dock fire station for the three weeks the oil tanks blazed, came to £800 – a staggering sum even by today's standards.

Five firemen were killed, and medical treatment was as follows: serious cases (hospital) 38; minor cases (eyes) 241; burns to hands, face and neck 180; sprains and strains 12; septic feet 2; foot treatment due to oil entering boots 560; cuts and abrasions 22; gastric cases 13.

The Llanreath depot contained 17 tanks with a total of 204,000 tons of oil or approximately 45,000,000 gallons. Eleven tanks were destroyed, representing a total of 33,000,000 gallons of oil lost.

An investigation into the effects the fire had on agriculture was undertaken, and an interim report subsequently published. This stated that from August 19th to the 28th, the wind's direction varied between north and north – west, with the result that oil and smoke were carried and deposited over a belt of land extending across South Pembrokeshire in a south-easterly direction, which became known as the "Oil Belt".

In this belt buildings, agricultural machinery, gate posts and vegetation of all kinds, were heavily bespattered and contaminated with oil. Produce of market gardens was entirely spoilt, and the leaves of such vegetables as sugar beet were severely damaged in the fields.

Serious losses of sheep occurred throughout the belt, and a number of cattle also died. The condition of surviving animals which had been on "oiled" pastures, was markedly reduced, and the milk yield dropped suddenly and excessively. The report disclosed that the weather had been very dry for many weeks prior to the bombing, and that the first appreciable amount of rain didn't fall until the night of September 19th-20th.

Persons whose property was affected by contamination were listed as: Mrs Jenner, Pennar; J. W. Phillips, 54 Military Road, Pennar; G. M. Donovan, 10 Ferry Road, Pennar; Reg Lewis, Glenavon, Pennar; R. W. Jones, West Grove; J. Ll. Morris, Brownslate; W. G. Wynne, Mellaston; J. W. Morris, Bowett; A. Hitchcox, Orielton Gardens; J. M. Thomas, West Orielton; A. H. Richards, Valasthill; L. B. Roberts, Lyserry; E. C. Roberts, Loveston; F. J. Jones, Sampson; W. James, Carew; W. Henton, Glebe, Bosherston; T. H. Griffiths, Style; and T. C. Murray, Buckspool.

A total of 223 sheep died, and referring to the effect of oil on animals the report declared "Within a few days after the bombing, sheep and cattle throughout the oil belt began to lose condition and became progressively and fairly rapidly emaciated. This loss of condition was quite obvious in October, even after supplementary feeding".

The milk yield dropped within three days after the bombing from one half to one third of the previous total. Owing to the excessively dry summer, the yield had been gradually diminishing, but such a sudden and severe drop could not be attributed to the same cause.

Under the heading "Financial Losses in the Affected Area", the report

Members of Pembroke Dock Fire Brigade being inspected – and congratulated – after the battle to save the six remaining tanks had been won. About a third of the brigade is shown here.
(Mrs Pat Phillips)

said "This matter was thoroughly gone into during the course of the investigation, and it is quite evident that the financial losses will seriously handicap food production in the area concerned. Some farmers have lost several years rent, and have been forced to purchase cake and other supplementary feeding stuffs to try to restore condition and milk production.

"Others cannot afford to buy artificial manure necessary for certain crops, and others again, who would have normally bought cows to keep up the milk supply, are now unable to do so. In view of the urgent necessity for food production of every kind at the present time, and of the impractability of producing even peacetime quantities in the area concerned owing to the losses, one would emphatically suggest that compensation would be sound investment on the part of the local authorities".

The Llanreath inferno left an indelible imprint on the minds of those who fought the fire. After the war a Midlands fireman wrote in the *Birmingham Weekly Post* "Though men from our contingent went on many other regional calls, none was quite like Pembroke Dock and the memory of it will forever remain vivid. They will remember not only the fire-fighting but other things, caught as it were, out of the corner of the eye.

The remaining tanks as they looked in 1980. Five years later they were demolished. In the background is the Barracks Hill.   *(Martin Cavaney)*

For instance, there was a naval representative, an amazing man, who each day made a tour of the tanks and walked across the tops of burning ones to test their strength. Then there was the little 100 gallon pump that was working when we got there, and was still going as strongly as ever after five continuous days".

The firemen also earned the admiration and respect of the men and women of Pembroke Dock, Pembroke and the immediate vicinity, and perhaps this was best summed up by Mrs Addie John, Beach Road, Llanreath.

She recalled "I had returned to the house to collect some belongings and saw a fireman, coated with oil from head to foot and almost asleep on his feet, coming up Llanreath hill from the beach. He was staggering all over the road like a drunken man. I offered him a cup of tea which he gladly accepted and then, with great difficulty, he pulled off his boots and removed his oilskins. I gave him rags and paraffin to clean up the worst and he washed himself thoroughly with hot water and soap.

"By then he was dazed and exhausted, and broke down and wept. I told him he could rest and handed him an old trousers and jacket. He fell into a deep sleep and when I woke him later he said he came from Tenby. He never did mention his name and I have long forgotten his face, but I shall never forget what he and his kind stood for in that long ago summer of 1940".

EPILOGUE

A number of people who knew him closely supplied information about Pembroke Dock's wartime fire chief Arthur Morris, and the remarks attributed to him, his Milford counterpart Matt Acornley and other brigade personnel mentioned in the narrative, are as accurate as could be remembered by men frequently in their close company and who shared the same risks and dangers.

One thing which struck me forcibly during numerous interviews I had 20 years ago with survivors of the Pembroke Dock and Pembroke brigades of 1940 was that after all that time resentment still smouldered over the exclusion of "Pomp" Morris from the awards list.

There is no doubt that Morris was a fireman's fireman, respected and much admired, not only by his own men but also by those from other brigades who came to know him. Frank John, Stanley Jones and Jack Philpin of Milford's wartime brigade, continued to insist over the years it was a grave miscarriage of justice that when the awards were drawn up by Tom Breaks, Morris was overlooked.

What also provoked anger was that not one local member of the various Pembrokeshire brigades – whose courage and fortitude was never in question – received an award. With the firemen of Pembroke Dock and Pembroke leading the way, Pembrokeshire personnel were first into the Llanreath depot after the bombing and the very last to leave when the blaze was finally extinguished. Understandably, the people of Milford Haven reacted with pride when it was announced that Matt Acornley and Horace Howarth had been honoured but neither was local, both originating from the North of England.

In addition to Mr Acornley, other George Medal recipients were: Robert John Knight, Auxiliary Fireman, Birmingham AFS; Fire Sergeant Daniel James Collins, Cardiff Fire Brigade; Sub-Officer William Brown and Leading Fireman Norman Groom, Cardiff AFS; Fire Sergeants William Victor Philpott and Ernest Smith, and Firemen Bertram Charles Ernest Arkell, Walter Bryant and Albert Victor Thomas, all of the Bristol Fire Brigade; Patrol Officers Maurice Charles Day, Frederick Charles Revelle and Lewis Jack Watts, Bristol AFS. An OBE for gallantry and meritorious service went to Maurice Clarke Sadler, Patrol Officer, Bristol AFS, and Alfred Richard Bridgeley Hart, Newport Fire Brigade. Hart was a former member of the Bristol Fire Brigade, which he joined in 1926. He left in April 1939 to become station officer at Newport.

The gallantry of Day, Revelle and Watts, of the Bristol AFS, is worthy of recall. Like Auxiliary Fireman Knight of Birmingham, Day and Revelle climbed a ladder to plug holes in the top of a tank through which burning oil was spewing. They succeeded, but were almost smothered and blinded in the process.

All these Bristol firemen won the George Medal with the exception of Patrol Officer Maurice Clarke Sadler, who was awarded the Medal of the Civilian Division of the Order of the British Empire. Ranks given are those held when the citation was published, not those held when the photograph was taken.

The awards were published in the 'London Gazette' of October 22nd 1940.

Left to right, seated: Fire Constable Bertram Charles Ernest Arkell; Fire Sergeant Ernest Smith; Fire Sergeant William Victor Philpott; Fire Constable Walter Bryant; Left to right, standing: Patrol Officer Frederick Charles Revelle; Patrol Officer Maurice Charles Day; Fire Constable Albert Victor Thomas; Patrol Officer Sadler; Auxiliary Fireman Jack Lewis Watts.   (Andy Stevens Collection)

Patrol Officer Maurice Clarke Sadler, OBE, pictured with his future wife, Betty, whom he married later in the war. Like other Bristol firemen he regarded the fire at Pembroke Dock as "the fire to end all fires".

(Andy Stevens Collection)

Watts was with two other men holding back a torrent of fire with their hoses. Two of the hoses failed and the fire swept forward. The chances of the single jet being able to contain it looked extremely slim and the three men were in grave danger of being overwhelmed, with other lives at risk as well. But Watts stood his ground and was able to check the fire until the arrival of reinforcements.

Bristol had 115 firemen at the Llanreath depot, which was about the combined strength of the Pembrokeshire brigades.

Every local fire brigade veteran interviewed in 1980 referred at some time or another to Tom Breaks, yet not one knew anything about his background.

Some years later I learned that two months after the oil tanks fire, when the Luftwaffe began its winter bombing offensive against Britain's provincial towns and cities, Tom Breaks was sent first to Coventry, and then Birmingham. Following the formation of the National Fire Service (NFS) on August 18th 1941, he was appointed chief regional fire officer for the northern region. Three years later – for what were described as "personal reasons" – he resigned this position and thereafter severed all connections with the fire service.

It was a dramatically sudden end to what had been a long, colourful and highly successful and rewarding career. He had followed his father into the fire service and in the First World War was awarded the Croix de Guerre for outstanding work with a military fire brigade in France. In 1935, when he commanded Sheffield Fire Brigade, then the sixth largest in Britain, he was appointed the youngest-ever President of the Institute of Fire Engineers.

Two years later there was much concern about the growing military might of Hitler's Germany, and he became the first ever Chief Inspector of the Fire Brigades Division at the Home Office. He was charged with the main responsibility of preparing a wartime fire service, and so when Britain declared hostilities with Germany on September 3rd 1939, it was thanks to Breaks and his Home Office staff that the nation had all the equipment it needed for the Auxiliary Fire Service. This was demonstrated during the Llanreath fire when an enormous amount of equipment destroyed by "boil-overs" was very quickly replaced.

Although he unexpectedly – and inexplicably – quit the service in 1944, it was a measure of the man's stature, and his many achievements, that 18 years later he was still considered worthy enough to be the subject for a "This is Your Life" programme on BBC Television, hosted by Eamonn Andrews.

Reg Haley, another former President of the Institution of Fire

Engineers, was a one-time colleague of Tom Breaks, and during a holiday visit to Pembroke Dock in the late 1980s, described him as being "tall and lean, with a Hitler-like moustache"! When Mr Haley called at the Pembroke Dock office of the *Telegraph*, he told me "Tom Breaks was a larger than life character who led from the front. He was a 24-hour-a-day, 365-days-a-year chief who never really required a deputy".

No one doubted Breaks leadership qualities during the tanks conflagration. What turned local firemen against him was that not one of their number was recognised in the awards list, and they were particularly aggrieved over the omission of Chief Arthur Morris.

Something surely happened to prompt the Home Office man to ignore the Pembroke Dock fire chief, but the reason will never be known now.

· ‖ ═╍•❖•╍═ · ─

Someone who followed with keen interest the *"Inferno 1940"* instalments when they appeared in the *Telegraph* in 1980, was Mr Trevor James of Pembroke, then living in London.

It was Mr James who told me the fascinating story of a meeting in Palestine 12 months after the war between his uncle, Lieutenant Colonel Tom Powell REME, and a Luftwaffe colonel who at that time was still a prisoner of the British, awaiting repatriation to Germany.

Mr James became acquainted with the facts about the German aviator back in 1947 when, as an army sergeant, he was sent to Iraq with a detachment of British troops. By chance his uncle was stationed there at the time and the two men arranged to get together. They spoke about home, and the savage battering Pembroke Dock received from German

In recent years a pleasant residential street in the Bufferland area of Pembroke Dock was named after the local fire chief of 1940, at the instigation of the town council. Members felt that the man who played such an important part in the drama of 60 years ago should be so honoured.

(John Evans)

aircraft during the war. It was then Lieutenant Colonel Powell confided that just 12 months previously he had met the Luftwaffe pilot who led the raid against the Llanreath oil tanks in 1940.

After learning that the British officer was from Pembroke Dock, the German told him that on that August day, while so many of their comrades were locked in aerial combat with RAF fighters over Southern England, he and his crew and the airmen in the accompanying Ju 88s, met with no resistance whatever. He also disclosed the hitherto unknown fact that shortly after dawn on the day of the raid, a lone German reconnaisance plane made a high-level run across Pembroke Dock to ascertain whether defensive cover had been provided for the town since previous visits by Luftwaffe aircraft. Within a couple of hours the pilot was back at his airfield in France with the re-assuring news that Pembroke Dock remained undefended. The order was then given for the assault against the tanks to go ahead that afternoon.

Lieutenant Colonel Powell died at Bridgend in 1970. Born in Pembroke Dock, he entered the dockyard there as an apprentice but joined the army following the 'yard's closure in 1926. He had a distinguished military career and saw much active service during the war years.

Mr Trevor James, now in his 70s, is still living in London.

In the 1990s Mrs Jennie Goddard, brought up in Pembroke Dock, was working in a tourist shop on the Isle of Sky when a party of German visitors arrived. One eventually approached her and asked where she hailed from because she didn't have a Scots accent?

When Mrs Goddard said "Wales", the German asked "What part?" to which she replied "A town called Pembroke Dock. I don't suppose you have heard of it?"

"But I have", the German retorted with a smile, "you see, my father was one of the airmen who bombed the oil tanks there in the war!" He then spread his hands into the air and said "Bang!"

I met Mrs Goddard when she was home on holiday in September 2000, and she said she still regretted not asking that German tourist for his name and address for the benefit of Pembrokeshire historians!

May Tobin, the Llanreath teenager mentioned in Chapter Three, escaped with severe shock after being blown up the passage-way of her home when the tank was hit. But luck deserted her the following year.

On the night of May 11th-12th 1941, Pembroke Dock was subjected to saturation bombing by a large force of enemy aircraft, and the Pier Hotel at the junction of Tremeyrick Street with London Road, received a direct hit. A number of people were killed and many more seriously wounded

Shortly before the 40th anniversary of the oil tanks raid these veterans of the Pembroke Dock and Pembroke brigades who fought the fire came together for this photograph at Llanreath. Behind them is the valley which separated the hamlet from the oil fuel depot, and the close proximity of the tanks is all too obvious. From the left are: Harry Baker, Eddie Jones, Bill Griffiths, Tom Gibby, Ronnie Campbell, George Fish, Charles Thomas, Jim Poldo, Len Haggar, Billy Neil, Jack Vincent and Alf Grieve. All are now deceased. *(Martin Cavaney)*

including May, who was working at the hotel that night. She lost the sight of her right eye, and spent several months in hospital, including some time at the skin-graft unit in Chepstow. The May 11th-12th blitz on Pembroke Dock occurred four days following her 19th birthday. She returned after the war to Llanreath and lived there until her death some years ago.

Harry Baker who, as section leader, was on duty at Pembroke Dock Fire Brigade headquarters on the afternoon the tanks were bombed, passed away in the early 1980s. When the tank erupted and the minutes ticked by without the siren sounding, it was Baker who shouted "If the ARP let the public down once more like this, I'll sound the bloody thing myself!" Some months later, when again there was no advance warning of a heavy air raid, Harry Baker carried out his threat – and was severely reprimanded. But his action undoubtedly saved a number of lives.

Councillor (later Alderman) J. R. Williams, who warned that he'd send a petition to the King signed by every person in Pembroke Dock if there

Fire hero Bob Knight, back at the site of the oil tanks where he won the George Medal.

Western Telegraph, September 30th, 1982

Fire hero returns to the scene of wartime oil tanks blaze

BY VERNON SCOTT

A second world war hero came back to Pembroke Dock on Sunday to visit the site where his bravery earned him the George Medal 42 years ago.

Bob Knight, now 72, was one of a large contingent of Birmingham fire brigade personnel sent to Pembroke Dock on August 21st, 1940, following the attack two days earlier, by German aircraft on the Admiralty oil tanks at Pennar.

Not long afterwards he volunteered for what was to be an exceptional feat of bravery, scaling a ladder placed against a burning oil tank in conditions of appalling danger to plug a hole from which scalding oil was gushing. Had the hole not been plugged the escaping oil would have become huge tongues of flame once the fire had reached it.

Bob Knight and his Midland colleagues, helped fight the tanks inferno for four days and nights before being hastily recalled to Birmingham which, by then, was being heavily blitzed by the Luftwaffe.

HOLIDAY

His wife Kathleen recalls: "When he got home I failed to recognise him. He was unwashed, unshaven. His uniform was scorched brittle. His eyes were badly burned and his hair, until then quite long and curly, had fallen out in a powder when he removed his cap after climbing the oil tank.

"He got home at six in the evening and by nine o'clock he was out fighting fires during one of the severest raids of the war on Birmingham."

Mr. and Mrs. Knight now live in retirement near Croydon, and for the last week they've been on holiday in Tenby staying at the Kinlock Hotel.

Bob contacted me asking if I could arrange for him to visit the tanks site for the first time since he was there with firefighters drawn from 22 different brigades all those years ago.

And thanks to the co-operation of Mr. Gwyn John, assistant services manager with South Pembrokeshire District Council, who holds the keys to the old oil tanks depot, the George Medal holder was able to inspect the site on Sunday morning.

He admitted later: "It gave me a very funny feeling to go back there. Brave men died fighting that tanks blaze and we all worked under unbelievably hazardous and frightening conditions. It was strange being there to see the site in clear, fresh air. All the time back in August 1940 you could hardly see a thing for smoke."

Next month another battle of a far different kind involving the Pennar oil tanks will commence.

Local councillors are strongly opposed to a Welsh Office proposal to use the tank depot for the disposal of oily waste in the event of a major tanker disaster off the Welsh coast.

A public inquiry will be held in Pennar on October 19th.

● Vernon Scott's book about the oil tanks fire, INFERNO 1940, is still available from the *Western Telegraph* price £2, post and packing 40p extra.

When George Medal holder George Knight of Birmingham returned to the tank site in 1982, he made front page news in the 'Western Telegraph'. (John Evans Collection)

95

was further delay in the building of public shelters in the town, became one of Pembrokeshire's best known public figures after the war. He had the double honour of being elected mayor of the ancient borough of Pembroke, and chairman of the county council. During an air raid on Pembroke Dock in the winter of 1940-41, he also sounded the siren because no "red alert" had been received. Like Harry Baker, the irrepressible 'JR' was hauled over the coals, but emerged from a meeting with incensed officials vowing "If need be, I'll do the same again!" He was a good example of the old saying "A man of character in peace, is a man of courage in war".

The oil tanks fire is remembered by some people for different reasons. For Harry Baker's daughter, Hannah, it led to romance. In the major shake-up that followed the tanks raid, hurried arrangements were made to provide Pembroke Dock with adequate defence and an anti-aircraft gun, manned by RAF personnel, was sited at Front Street close to the Baker's home. George Young from Bournemouth was posted to Pembroke Dock as a member of the gun crew, and met Hannah. They eventually married and still live in Front Street today.

The Royal Navy also built up its strength at Pembroke Dock, and one of the first ratings to arrive was Eddie Lomas from Derbyshire. He met Betty Davies, the young ambulance driver from Pennar, and they later married.

Up to the time of his death a Pembroke wartime auxiliary fireman, Ronnie Campbell, still had an un-opened wage packet he received from Pembroke Borough Council for his services at the oil tanks fire. It contained an old ten shillings note, some half crowns and amounted to less than one pound.

Such was the price of the blood, toil, tears and sweat endured by the valiant men who fought the great fire at Pembroke Dock.

* · ·:·—:●D●C●●:●:—·· ·

Bob Knight of the Birmingham Fire Brigade, whose valour during the fire earned him the George Medal, returned to the site for the first time in September 1982.

After being conducted around, he admitted "Being back here has left me with a very perculiar feeling. Brave men died fighting that blaze, and we all worked under unbelievably hazardous and frightening conditions. It is strange to see the site in clear, fresh air. All the time back in August-September 1940 you could hardly see your hand in front of you for smoke".

Birmingham left Pembroke Dock before the other English brigades because by then their city was under heavy attack by the Germans. Bob's homecoming was described by his wife Kathleen: "When he came in through the door I failed to recognise him. He was unwashed and unshaven. His uniform was scorched brittle. His eyes were badly burned and his hair, quite long and curly before he went to Pembroke Dock, had gone completely. It fell out in a powder when he removed his headgear after climbing the ladder to plug the hole at the top of the burning tank. He got home at six in the evening and by 9pm, despite his weariness and travel fatigue, was out with the others who'd been to Pembroke Dock, fighting fires in one of the severest raids of the war on Birmingham".

In terms of death and destruction to property, the oil tanks raid could not be compared with the dreadful bombing Pembroke Dock would endure over the next 12 months.

But it was the first major air attack of the war on the town and, as such, caused immense damage to civilian morale. Yet it also served one very important purpose. It brought home to the War Office that the Germans regarded Pembroke Dock as a prime military target, and reaction was swift.

Within six weeks of the attack on the tanks Pembroke Dock – and the Milford Haven waterway as a whole – was ringed by anti-aircraft guns, searchlight batteries, and barrage balloons.

Work also began in the early winter of 1940 on the construction of an airfield at Angle which was ready for occupation by the following summer. One of the famous Battle of Britain squadrons, number 32, was first to

Spitfires of 312 (Czech) Squadron scramble at RAF Angle in 1942. RAF Angle was established as a direct result of the oil tanks raid which exposed the complete lack of defences in such an important military area.

(Squadron Leader Tony Liskutin, DFC, AFC)

serve there, arriving in June. The airfield's initial role was that of a fighter base for the protection of the Milford Haven-Pembroke Dock area, but duties later included convoy protection patrols.

The remaining Llanreath oil tanks were demolished in 1985 – ironically by a specialist firm from Germany. Today the site, together with the adjacent Barracks Hill, forms South Pembrokeshire Golf Club's attractively laid out 18 hole course, from where the panoramic view of Milford harbour never fails to impress local and visiting players.

The only reminder of the momentous events there 60 years ago is a memorial to the five Cardiff firemen, immaculately cared for by golf club officials, and located close to the clubhouse entrance. Since its unveiling on the 55th anniversary of the raid in 1995, a service has been held on the site every August, attended by representatives of the present day Mid and West Wales Fire Brigade, and veterans of the great fire, including three Cardiff stalwarts, Hubert "Buzzer" Reynolds, William G. Kirby, and John Walsh. Relatives of the Cardiff firemen who perished also travel to Pembroke Dock for the service which, because of the historical significance of the golf club site, is to continue as an annual event.

Pictured at the 1999 service at the memorial to the men who died are veterans who fought the fire 59 years earlier: Ted Owens and Bill Griffiths, Pembroke Dock; Wyndham Scourfield, Narberth; Brian Jones, Carmarthen; John Carey, Swansea; Hubert Reynolds, Bill Kirby and John Walsh, all of Cardiff. A week after this photograph was taken, Bill Griffiths (leaning on stick) passed away.

(John Evans)

Fire chiefs, clergy, tanks fire veterans, relatives of the Cardiff firemen who were killed, South Pembrokeshire Golf Club members and local friends joined together for the 1999 memorial service by the memorial stone. (*John Evans*)

In this group at the August 2000 memorial service are veterans Wyndham Scourfield, John Walsh, Bill Kirby and Hubert Reynolds, fire chiefs Mr Ronnie King and Mr A. D. Martin, the officiating clergyman, the Rev Canon Randolph Thomas, and the fire brigades colour party. (*John Evans*)